Caring   Love   Respect

Dignity   Sensitivity

PERSON-SHINE
The Power of Brightening Our Lives

The process of reaching out to others with
positive words and actions of DIGNITY, LOVE, RESPECT,
SENSITIVITY AND CARING,
making the lights of their worlds brighter!

Kenneth H. Mills, Ed.D.

Darlene Ann (Hanson) Mills, RN
Design Consultant & Critical Analyst

Cindi Thiede, Ph.D.
Editor

Ms. Darlene Mills
N6160 Kapur Dr.
Sheboygan Fls., WI 53085

© 2006

Kenneth H. Mills

Other Books by Kenneth H. Mills:
(with coauthor Dr. Judith E. Paul)
Applied Visual Merchandising, 3rd Edition
Applied Visual Merchandising
Create Distinctive Displays
Successful Retail Sales
Applied Visual Merchandising, 2nd Edition
Checker-Cashier

Mills, Kenneth H.

    Person-shine : the power of brightening our lives / Kenneth H. Mills. -- 1st ed. -- Sheboygan, WI : Person-Shine Publishing, 2006.

        p. ; cm.

        ISBN-13: 978-0-9778327-0-5
        ISBN-10: 0-9778327-0-8
        "The process of reaching out to others with positive words and actions of dignity, love, respect, sensitivity and caring, making the lights of their worlds brighter!"

        1. Positive psychology. 2. Influence (Psychology)
    3. Interpersonal relations. 4. Self-help techniques.
        I. Title.

BF204.6 .M55 2006   2006901515
150.19/8--dc22   0604

PERSON-SHINE

Send a card, make a call
Reach out to someone in need.
Celebrate other's specialness,
Plant the Person-Shine seed.

There's a place deep within the heart.
The tenderest, most fragile place.
It can be deeply hurt or sunshine brushed
Causing smile or frown on our face.

We don't always share it with others.
We don't always let others know,
The negative feelings, fears or hurts
We try not to let them show.

But if someone cares enough
If they want to share their light
If they want to reach beyond their needs
They can make others' heart places bright.

Each day we have the choice
Of how we're going to act and feel.
We reach inside our inner soul
Search for the light—say a prayer as we kneel.

Next we try to kindle our heartlight
So we can welcome each day with a positive view
We know we have the power within
To use our specialness in all that we do.

If our inner light burns brightly
If we've chosen the positive road
We can be a mighty force in others' lives
And lighten others' loads.

We can give them golden presence,
Asking how they really feel.
We can ask the second question
And listen to their points of view.

We can let them know they're valued
In so many simple ways,
Which will lift high their self-esteem
Touch their heartplace and brighten both of our days.

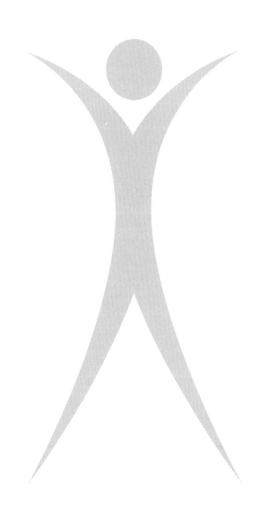

DEDICATION

This book contains what I strongly and deeply believe in how we should treat one another. It is to honor those who have defined and taught me those beliefs. It is my legacy to my friends, children and grandchildren, and those to come. There is only one person, besides God, who has given me the total support, love, inspiration, confidence, faith, commitment and perseverance, every moment of her life, that allowed me to travel my journey, learning and trying to live those beliefs...Darlene Ann (Hanson) Mills. Her unselfish, total devotion to me, our marriage, our friends and children...and now our grandchildren, has been and is unwavering. She is my greatest critic but only to help me become a better professional, person, partner and friend. Because of these and many other gifts that she has given to our love partnership, our life's journey has been sunshine during the good times and brilliant rainbows in the challenging times.

Darlene's presence in my life is what air is to lungs, sunshine is to hearts, soil and rain are to beautiful flowers and inspiration is to the poet, the artist, the composer, the architect and the builder. She always has been and is truly my guiding supportive spirit and the sunshine of my life. I have had my special moments when I was greater than I could have ever dreamed! During each of those moments from doctorate, to author, to president, to father and friend, I always realized that those moments would never have been possible without Darlene's special gifts.

To dedicate means to devote one's self to some special work or cause; to set apart for any special use. As Darlene has so done by devoting her life to me, making my life special, it is very fitting to dedicate this book to her...a great mother, grandmother, professionally multitalented nurse, faith partner, daughter, sister, mother-in-law, neighbor, child of God, wife and friend...giving her signature love gifts of caring and service!

Thank you Darlene for this wonderful journey, for the music you have given my heartsong. Hugs and Love...God bless, peace, love and Joy!

ACKNOWLEDGMENTS

I wish to thank: Glen Taylor for his review of the manuscripts and his kind, generous and thoughtful words in the foreword; Dr. Cindi Thiede, personal editor, for her intellect, analytical talents and research ability and especially for her leadership in creating the Person-Shine Growth Guide; Darlene Ann (Hanson) Mills for always being such a firm critic of my work, for leading the design team which selected the cover and Hugs logo designs for this book, for her participation as a member of the panel of experts, and for hosting the weekend workshop for that group; The panel of experts, listed by name and title in the appendix, for their time and effort in carefully reviewing, ranking and critically commenting on the original forty-two manuscripts and their participation in the weekend workshop, (the author used about ninety-five percent of the team's recommendations) where they reviewed the newly revised manuscript and made further major meaningful recommendations; The manuscript reviewers, listed by name and title in the appendix, for their time and effort in critically reviewing the book and growth guide manuscripts, resulting in the author's making considerable changes and refinements; The many people from all walks of life who read the manuscripts and offered their personal quotes, listed in the appendix, about the material; Jim Pierce who, in addition to being a member of the panel of experts, inspired the author to create the Person-Shine guidelines in 1982; Troy and Lisa Anderson, owners of White Ivy Design, who were co-developers of the Hugs logo, assisted in the book cover design and integrated both of the designs into the manuscripts; my parents, Amelia and Harlem Mills; our children Mary Theodoroff, Mark Mills and Ken Mills, their spouses Jim, Jennifer and Darlene, who have taught me and given me love and support beyond belief; the many friends, mentors, teachers, leaders and colleagues who have taught me, counseled me, supported me and loved me as I've made my way along this wonderful journey called LIFE. Lastly and most powerfully, my dear Lord and Savior for being a constant companion, a giver of blessings beyond anyone's wildest dreams and a Teacher of love, kindness, forgiveness and caring. His forever sunshine is always there with me each day if I but remember to open my heart, my mind and my soul and accept his magnificent loving Presence.

TABLE OF CONTENTS

Hugs Logos   Sample Selections

FOREWORD

The day I first met Ken Mills, I immediately liked him as a leader and a friend. He was positive about everything in life. You could feel his compassion and interest when visiting with him. As our friendship has grown over the years, I have admired the unique qualities that Ken possesses. These attributes have made him the special successful person in the lives of all who have come to know him.

Through his teaching, Ken shares the experiences and values that have guided him. PERSON-SHINE is the process Ken found that reaches out to others with positive words and actions, brightening each individual's world. The book is filled with practical, down-to-earth advice mixed with stories that produce value to the reader.

Through Ken's insight, each of us can learn habits that will not only enrich our lives, but those around us whom we love and care about.

I enjoy the competition and the growing experiences involved in each of my businesses. My goal for each business is to have them be #1 in their field. I have learned it is small improvements that make the difference between being good and being great. The ideas that Ken uses in PERSON-SHINE provide a toolkit a leader or manager can use to help individuals find the instruments necessary to compete in today's ever-changing environment.

Glen Taylor
Chairman, Taylor Corporation; Owner, Minnesota Timberwolves

INTRODUCTION

"There is a destiny that makes us brothers: None goes his way alone: All that we send into the lives of others comes back onto our own."

Edwin Markham

I have over thirty years of experience in consulting, writing and leadership positions. I have been fired, awarded, recognized, criticized and celebrated. All of these and the abounding research tells me that the individual is important, of great worth and should be treated appropriately. No one should have the power or the right to demean or to mistreat anyone in any way. My mission in life is to recognize and hold up the power and value of the individual. My passion in life is to celebrate the positive, eliminate the negative, and bring mental sunshine to others, wherever and whenever possible.

The mission of this book is to emotionally and dramatically remind us of the immense value of each person in our many worlds and of the power we have to brighten their lives, and in so doing our lives! I call it PERSON-SHINE. It is the process of reaching out to others with positive words and actions, brightening their worlds. The Person-Shine process is based on twelve guidelines that provide a pathway to improve how we treat others. We choose to what extent we will be committed to:

- React or Respond
- Valuing Each Person
- Give Back, Give Away
- Take Time to Care
- Place Priority on Giving Rather than Recognition
- Listen to Others' Words and Feelings
- Only Ask if You're Going to Listen
- Say You're Wrong, Say You're Sorry
- Being Positive is Personally Powerful
- Care About Others' Whole Lives

- Verbalize Your Feelings, Visualize Your Thoughts.
- Celebrate, Applaud and Remember

Reflections are also included at the end of each chapter to provide some "food for thought" and possible actions. The accompanying Personal-Organizational Growth Guide gives additional practical ways to learn and apply the guidelines.

My wife Darlene and I have three married children and eight grandchildren ranging in age from one to fifteen. We have been married for over forty years and it is true that our love is stronger today than it has ever been. However, we have made our share of mistakes in parenting, have had and have our marriage relationship struggles, and have had and have other challenges. We agree, as do workshop participants, that these guidelines have been and continue to be a pathway to brighten the worlds of families, friends and all others in our centers of influence.

I decided to use a people driven process to strengthen the contents of this book. It began with writing several manuscripts that fit the twelve guidelines, using well-researched information, workshop results and experience of other leaders. Next a Panel of Experts (names listed in the appendix) individually reviewed the forty-two manuscripts ranked them and offered suggestions for improvement. Third, a leading researcher and objective writer joined the team as editor. Fourth, the material was revised into a manuscript. The panel of experts was invited to participate in a workshop to review, discuss and offer recommendations for improving the newly revised manuscript. Finally a new manuscript draft was individually reviewed by authors, ceos and other professionals (names listed in the appendix). Their suggestions were considered and a final manuscript was prepared and piloted in a company training setting. An additional team headed by Darlene finalized an illustration theme, working with a graphics designer and illustrator.

The official, copyrighted HUGS logo is being formally announced with the publication of this book. The two colors as shown in the back of the book phrases that match those colors—blue for emotional support and yellow for celebration messages. They were designed by Darlene Mills, Christina Theodoroff, Troy and Lisa Anderson of White Ivy Graphic Art and Design and Ken Mills. The logos, with appropriate phrases, have been integrated into each chapter. Samples of the various HUGS logos have been included in the back of the book. An order blank has been included for those wishing additional logos.

Readers are invited to submit stories that fit one or more of the guidelines. These stories may be selected for inclusion in future Person-Shine publications. Interested parties should write to the publisher following the procedure given at the end of this book.

May you learn from the guidelines, enjoy and be moved by the stories and choose more often to use the power within you to brighten others' worlds.

"Mental sunshine will cause the flowers of peace, happiness, and prosperity to grow upon the face of the earth. Be a creator of mental sunshine."

Author unknown

CHAPTER 1

THE POWER OF ONE

"You see things; and you say, 'Why?' But I dream things that never were; and I say, 'Why not?'"

George Bernard Shaw

Negativism/Positivism

Negativism is such a powerfully destructive energy force! It is present in all our lives, every day, in some way. It can overpower us and drag us down. We can overcome negativism if we have a strong enough desire and commitment to value those around us. It's our choice. It isn't easy. In fact, most of the time it's very difficult. Surveys from hundreds of seminar participants I've worked with on positive/negative behavior agreed how hard it is to remain positive!

One theory proposed (author unknown) a few years ago, underscores the power of negative and positive behavior and the opportunity we have to motivate others to exhibit positive behavior. The author of this theory proposes that in any department, group or organization, ten percent of the people are positive, fifteen percent are negative and seventy-five percent may go either way, depending on what influences them on any given day. Those individuals who wish to brighten other people's worlds by exhibiting positive behavior can support the ten percent, may be able to modify the fifteen

17

percent and can have a significant impact on the seventy-five percent. These people are POSITIVE CHAMPIONS, because they try to do the best they can each and every day!

These POSITIVE CHAMPIONS bring personal sunshine into otherwise ordinary, maybe even dreary worlds; rainbows where negative storms are blowing and churning and a realization to others that no matter the cause, the background, or the experience, we can find a positive side, a positive view. Some call it seeing the "glass half full." I say it's much stronger, more vivid than that. But it's not easy. It's very difficult for us to be positive if we feel negative forces. The research indicates that negativism may come from a number of sources such as aging, physical and mental health, dissatisfaction with work careers, financial hardship, feeling trapped in our lives, and loss of control for many reasons. Difficult yes, but not impossible! Note: Being positive doesn't mean that we ignore the negative within us or that we can simply wish it away by pretending it doesn't exit. It means always choosing to look for the positive and use it to overcome the negative.

Positive Champion Jerry Lewis
Jerry Lewis, worldwide leading humanitarian, comedian, author, educator, film actor, producer and director, and Broadway star, has defined the "power of one!" Coming from humble beginnings he rose to stardom early in his life and succeeding in his quest for excellence, he positively touched the lives of hundreds of millions of people through his:
...movies (acting the beloved underdog,often touching his audiences with humor and song, and always winning in the end).
...stage performances (with song, dance, story and skit both with and without Dean Martin bringing audiences to their feet).
...never to be equaled fund-raising efforts in leading the development of the Muscular Dystrophy Association from its

infancy as a local agency to world-wide recognition through the annual MDA Labor Day Telethon.

I am one but of the hundreds of millions whose lives he's touched—this is my story! Jerry has been one of the primary people who taught me the "power of one" as I followed his personal and professional life over the years:

...As a child, with my family going through tough times, his movies have taken me to places of laughter and joy, places where everything turns to sunshine in the end. They supported what my parents taught me about looking for the rainbows in life.

...As one of my childhood heroes, later in life when I heard that he was touring the country and would be appearing in Chicago, I invited him to speak at my college in southern Wisconsin. He accepted my invitation and spent four hours on campus meeting with people and giving a faculty/staff in-service. As he left the campus, giving me his personal home number, he said "I could contact him whenever I needed him." I HAVE AND HE HAS ALWAYS BEEN THERE FOR ME. I realized later that his visit would end up in a never-ending friendship.

...As a Nobel nominee. Wanting to give back for what he had done for me I searched for and dreamed about ways I could return, in the same emotional measure, what he gave me during his visit. After sending cards and gifts for a couple of years, I finally came upon the avenue I would use—nominate him for the NOBEL PEACE PRIZE. After researching and writing the nomination paper and with the support of a local legislator (only national elected government officials or past Nobel Peace Prize Winners can actually submit a nomination), I submitted the nomination. The nomination was accepted in Norway. He didn't win, but he was the first entertainer ever to be nominated. Jerry called me from Las Vegas between performances and said, "Ken, what have you done to me? I have received hundreds of congratulation cards, letters and phone calls. No man has ever done this much for me!" Instantly, the strong aching need to give back left my stomach. The MDA office also called later and said the announcement of the nomination had substantially increased the giving that year to help "Jerry's Kids!" His generous friendship caused me to try to touch others' lives more deeply and more often. We have helped each other during challenging times in our lives, which is how friendships are formed.

Jerry Lewis has met and positively lived through many challenges! He absolutely never gives up. He always finds a way to land on his feet and somehow find the sunshine amid life's clouds. He has dramatically improved the worldwide "human condition!" By his actions, he daily lives the belief that each of us can make a positive difference. His life is a sterling example of "the power of one!" History will clearly show him to be a positive champion!

Positive Champion Mattie Stepanek

Mattie Stepanek, author of the New York Times bestseller, Journey Through Heartsongs, along with his mother had muscular dystrophy. Two of his brothers have died from the disease. Mattie died at the age of thirteen on June 22, 2004. He appeared on the Oprah and Larry King Shows, he was a special ambassador for the Muscular Dystrophy Association and annually appeared on the MDA Telethon. He met with President Carter and many other celebrities. His message was simple. "Count your blessings, value others, realize there is a powerful and caring God, appreciate each moment, each breath, each flower, and listen to your heartsong."

Positive Champion Dave Pelzer

Dave Pelzer, author of A Boy Called It, The Lost Boy, and A Man Called Dave, shares his journey. Dave's story is about escaping the cruelty of abuse by his mother in his teens. Today, he is a positive, caring man who harbors no bitterness and speaks about celebrating what we have.

Both Mattie and Dave have reasons to be negative, but they

are not. In fact, they are positive models, heroes if you will, of how we should live our lives—even though we'll always have struggles. They have found their personal sunshine, their rainbows in life's storms and the positive in their worlds. By sharing their lives with us they have brightened our worlds and shown us how we can be positive and brighten others' worlds. They are positive champions! We can be too!

Each of us can find the positive and overcome the negative whenever and wherever it exists. Many people model that behavior by overcoming the negative forces and remaining positive. PERSON-SHINE is based on the power each person has to be positive and to brighten other's worlds. The following stories are additonal examples of the "power of one".

Alexandra Scott of Philadelphia—The Power of One at any Age

This is a story about a seven year-old girl who has cancer and has undergone surgery and chemotherapy since she was four years old. When she was four and in the hospital receiving a stem cell transplant, her mother reluctantly (because of her condition) agreed to let her set up a lemonade stand to raise money for the hospital. Alexandra said that she wanted to help the hospital. A couple of weeks later, in the middle of heavy rain, on her third day, she raised $14,000. She has now raised over 1.2 million dollars to date. The power of one is incredible!

Senior Orphans Never Alone Again in Lakeland, Florida

While traveling to Orlando, my wife and I happened to stay at Jameson Inn in Lakeland, Florida. On the wall was a plaque entitled "Senior Orphans" with a 2002 date. Upon inquiry, the manager explained that the motel received it for participating at a local nursing home and a nearby church program. It seems that one day the pastor was approached by someone from the nursing home to give a funeral for a deceased senior citizen because the gentleman had no one. He was totally alone. How sad, he thought, that the person had lived his entire life and now, at the end, in his golden years, there was no one there for him. The pastor thought and prayed for a time about what he could do and figured there must be others like him. A vision came to him as to how he could help. He would find a person who was elderly and alone and "adopt" him or her. Thus began the Senior Orphans Program! Seniors are being adopted in the Lakeland community. Their adopted families add joy, laughter and love to their lives by their visits and family gatherings. And when they breathe their last breath, they have their adopted family at their bedside to hold their hands, close their eyes, and say goodbye, as the family members' tears of compassion and love flood their eyes. Their hearts are filled with the joy of knowing that they gave comfort and love to their new family member, who would otherwise have had no one. The program is growing in Lakeland and perhaps it will, one day, cover the entire country! The power of one!

Someone once said, "if we give too much respect to our problems we may kill or diminish our faith in possibilities." The power of positive thinking and living is immense. It is energy producing. It can give us hope for tomorrow in challenging times, increased motivation to brighten our worlds in good times and a clear picture of our blessings, our gifts, all of the time.

Person-Shine is one way we can brighten the world within us by sharing that light with others!

A positive Fire may be ignited within us, like the striking of a match, filling our life's journey with pathways of light, and brightening the lives around us...or it may not...it's our choice. The power is within us!

Kenneth H. Mills

Reflections

1. Who in our life has been or is a positive champion? How has their behavior impacted our life?

2. Can we describe a difficult challenge in our life that we faced positively and overcame? How did we feel at that time, no matter how long it lasted? What was the impact on us or our life since? On others' lives?

3. View a movie or read a book about the power of one. For example the movie, *Rudy,* or Dave Pelzer's books.

4. What is our greatest relationship goal in life as experienced in our jobs/career, our family and our friendships? Can we write it down? Have we achieved it? If so how might we celebrate it? If not, what can we do to achieve it?

MAY YOU FEEL MY SUPPORT

CHAPTER 2
THE COMMITMENT

"On every day everyone in the world should do at least one nice thing for others. Doing so can help each person believe in himself or herself more fully."

Mattie J.T. Stepanek

The Choice

If we want to be positive, if we want to brighten others' worlds and our own, and if we are to be successful, we must make a commitment to do so. Just like commitments to quit smoking or drinking, or to lose weight, this commitment requires emotional strength and practice. It's our choice. Noted author on positivism, Dr. Victor Frankl, reminds us of this in his writings. He believed that attitude is the only disability. He remembered living in concentration camps with others. The men would walk through the huts comforting others, giving away their last piece of bread. They may have been few in number, but they offer sufficient proof that everything can be taken away from a man but one thing—the human freedom to choose one's attitude in any given set of circumstances.

Inner and Other Directed Leadership

All it takes for evil people to succeed is for good people to do nothing! These paraphrased words from the German Nazi days, when Jewish people were being persecuted, tell us of the great harm in doing nothing. But we also have great power to choose to stand up and speak out for others. Perhaps it's an extreme example and yet it makes a dramatic point for situations we face almost every day regarding supporting others. We may be faced with the decision of supporting someone in their presence or absence, because it's the right thing to do. We exercise "inner-directed leadership" when we make the decision to speak up and "other-directed leadership" when we act and cause others to exhibit positive behavior. To do so certainly may brighten many worlds as is evidenced in this true story told before an audience of about 300 people at a retirement celebration.

Speaking Up, Not Always an Easy Choice
People in the audience had been invited to walk to a microphone in the middle of the room if they wished to offer stories about the celebrant. Chuck Adamson approached the microphone and said,

> Darlene and Ken came to visit my wife Caroll and I shortly after we had retired and moved to Arkansas. On the afternoon of their arrival we had been invited to a cocktail party with about twenty other guests. Ken and Darlene accompanied us to the party. Soon after everyone had arrived, had their drinks and hors d'oeuvres in hand, someone mentioned the name of a man in Mankato and made a negative comment about him. Immediately two or three others added more negative comments. Then another two or three added comments until most of the twenty people had spoken. After listening for about fifteen minutes Darlene spoke up and said, 'we know this man. He is a member of our Bible study group and a friend'. After a few seconds that seemed like several minutes someone else made a positive comment about the

gentleman. Then two or three others spoke. Soon the entire tone of the discussion turned around. This is the first time that I have publicly shared this story. I want to add that I hope that I'm a friend of Darlene's because I know that whether I'm present or not no one will speak negatively about me in her presence.

Three interesting comments reflect the importance of this episode. First, it shows the power of one positive person in a group who has the courage to speak up and speak out. Second, Darlene is somewhat shy and a very sensitive person, so it was very difficult for her to speak without knowing most of the rest of the group and what they might think about her. Third, it shows how natural and easy it is to be negative, to go along with a group when cutting someone down.

Tools to Support our Commitment

If we choose to make a commitment and be effective in brightening others' worlds, and in so doing brighten our own, we'll need to use some kind of tools or guidelines. We need to understand that we each have major strengths and weaknesses, which will be with us forever as Buckingham and Clifton stated in their book, Now Discover Your Strengths. They believe that because they will never go away we should work to manage our weaknesses and enhance (celebrate) our strengths. The twelve Person-Shine guidelines listed in the introduction and described in succeeding chapters, along with reinforcing stories, will help us to enhance our strengths and manage our weaknesses as we work to live more positive lives. HOWEVER, WHETHER WE CHOOSE TO DO SO OR NOT IS ALWAYS OUR CHOICE!

I invite us to make the commitment; to work harder to brighten others' worlds and in so doing, brightening our light, and to be better inner-directed and other-directed leaders!

"Be proactive. Proactive people and organizations are self-aware; accept responsibility for their own actions; don't blame and accuse others when things go wrong; work continuously within their circle of influence; and change and develop themselves first in order to have greater influence with others"

Stephen Covey

Reflections

1. View the movie, *The Miracle Worker* or *Patch Adams*. Read <u>Awakenings</u> by Oliver Sacks. These real life stories dramatize commitment in the most powerful form.

2. Think about one act that we've committed to brighten someone's world in the past week? How did it make us feel? How did the recipient respond?

3. Focus on only the good news or human interest stories in the media for several days. Be specific.

4. What might we do this coming week to brighten someone's world? Be specific.

5. Ask ourselves the question, "do we want to make a stronger commitment to brightening others' worlds?" If so, what kind of goal or goals do we want to set to do so? How do we want to verbalize that commitment? For example, a person I know uses a "relationship calendar." It has large blank spaces by each date. She plans a month ahead, and writes in some of the dates "brightening behaviors" like names of friends to contact, birthdays, and so on.

THE POWER OF HUGS IS MIGHTY ©

Philosophical Guidelines

Make the Commitment

You must review your own personality characteristics, admit that you love yourself and that you can care enough for others to put them first. This means consciously saying to yourself, perhaps even writing down, "I am going to practice PERSON-SHINE. I will make other individuals' worlds brighter—even when I feel low, even when I doubt the progress I've made or the impact I've had on others, even when I feel negative reactions. Most of all, during those times I will remind myself of my commitment to and the attributes of PERSON-SHINE. I can and will make a positive difference! It is my choice and I choose to help others to realize their great value to themselves and those around them."

CHAPTER 3

GUIDELINE 1
"REACT OR RESPOND"

"How far you go in life depends on your being tender with the young, compassionate with the aged, sympathetic with the striving, and tolerant of the weak and the strong, because someday in life you will have been all of these."

George Washington Carver

It's All About Being Sensitive

We should recognize that we must love ourselves first! Second, we want to love and care about others. Next, we reach out to those around us. It is important that we take the time to listen to others' feelings, be sensitive to their situations and give them support. We ask our co-workers, spouse, neighbors or friends about their feelings. We offer words and actions to support them, rather than reacting to their words or behavior in terms of our feelings, experiences and emotions at a specific time. If someone gives us a gift and we give one back, that's *reacting*. If someone yells at us and we yell back, that is *reacting*. But if someone yells at us and we stop to think about and find out what is going on in their lives, be sensitive to their situation and support them, that is *responding*.

The following true stories are dramatic examples of *responding,* not *reacting!*

Supervisor John

John, supervisor of a department of forty-five people, asked each employee to submit written goals. He received them from forty-four of the forty-five people. Next, if necessary, he individually met with those department members to discuss and revise their goals and finally approve each of their plans. For three weeks he sent reminders to Bill. He also spoke privately to Bill, telling him that he needed to submit his goals. Reaching the end of his patience, John asked to meet one more time with Bill. John said, "Bill, you are a valued employee. Your record is unblemished. You were promoted from a staff level to an assistant supervisor position just four weeks ago. Asking for your goals was the first request for anything in writing from you. I want to help you do well in your new role but you must do your part. Now, please tell me how I can help you. Then, let's agree on a date when I can expect to receive your plan."

Bill rose from his chair and turned to leave the office without saying a word. Just as he was about to open the door he turned and whispered, "I don't know how to write. In my twenty years I have never had to do more than fill in numbers on printed forms. The few times I had to write something out, I would find a way to take it home and have my wife do it for me. I haven't done my plan because I'm ashamed of my problem and was afraid I would be fired." The rest of the story is that he enrolled in writing classes and remained in his position. John tells this story with Bill's permission to remind him to be sensitive to each person's world and to respond accordingly–NOT REACT!

The Gift Tool that Can Improve any Relationship

The second story is about Darlene and Ken's "Gift." When Darlene and Ken had been married for several years, they came to the realization that their marriage really needed some help. Their differences were great and their weaknesses were serious. They attempted to find a beginning point, something they could build on. They agreed to begin using the *gift tool* to start the journey toward a better relationship. The gift tool is a powerful way for a person to do an unselfish act by giving a gift to the other person. Ken chose to center on one example of his negative behavior–something that bugged for Darlene twenty years. She wanted him to take the garbage out to the curb the night before it was to be picked up. Ken preferred doing it the next morning. So, to please Darlene, Ken took the garbage out Sunday night rather then Monday morning and risk missing the pickup. Knowing how much they had argued about this, Ken decided to act. He knew that this was the perfect time and place to begin using the gift tool. So, at 9:00 p.m. on a cold Sunday night in February, Ken took the garbage out and as he came back into the house he walked over to Darlene and said, "That's my gift to you because I love you!" He did that the following Sunday and the next and the next.

Darlene liked Ken's changed behavior so much that she thought she would try it. After ironing his clothes–something she was so tired of doing week in and week out for some twenty years–mundane task that it was, she pinned a note on them as she placed them in the closet. It said, "My gift to you, because I love you!"

Ken and Darlene have been using the Gift tool for more than fifteen years because it works. It is so simple! It is not how much we give, but how much love we put into the doing and giving of the Gift! It is being sensitive to and responding to the other person's needs.

The First Name on the List
Lisa and Jerry had been happily married for about fifteen years when we entered their lives. They had four very young, healthy children. They were a very close, loving family. Lisa's friends and Jerry all described her as an expressive, caring,

spiritual, giving and highly organized person. She and her family were deeply involved in their church's activities. Almost everyone in the 1500 family church knew Lisa and liked her a lot. Their life was perfect, filled with much joy. Then one day tragedy struck! Lisa had not been feeling well for a while and decided to see her doctor. After going through several tests the doctor told her the shocking news. She had cancer! It was in an advanced stage and the doctor said that she would not have long to live. After fighting it for over a year, with chemo drugs, she lost the struggle and died, leaving a husband and four children! Consistent with her strong spiritual and giving nature, she made a video for her family and friends. It was played, at her request, the day of the funeral. As one might expect there was not a dry eye in the entire church. Her daughter, the oldest of the four children, sang a song celebrating her mom's life. Her unselfish love didn't end with her death, and so begins, "the rest of the story."

It seems that Jerry was a great provider, but Lisa handled all the finances, children's schedules and organizing vacations. Knowing this and wanting to be helpful, Lisa made a list of single women who she thought would be good and loving spouses for Jerry. It so happened that after Lisa's death Jerry received a call from a woman named Mona, who lived in another town. She had been close to Jerry and Lisa for many years. She wanted to know if she could help, as she had heard that parishioners from their church had signed up to be at Jerry's home each school day, to make breakfast and help get the children ready for school. She ended up helping a lot and as the family settled into their new routines and as some of the sadness lifted, she and Jerry began to do things as a couple. This sharing time turned into dating. They got married several months later. You may have guessed by now that Mona was on the list that Lisa had made...IN FACT, SHE WAS THE FIRST NAME ON THE LIST! Lisa had been deeply sensitive to Jerry's needs, even before he knew what they were. She was very unselfish, thinking only of him and the children, and *responded.*

Mona Added Another Dramatic Chapter of *Responding* in this Story

The day of the wedding Mona presented a special gift, especially for Jerry, but also for the children from both families, the friends of both families and for Lisa. As she and Jerry were standing at the altar and just before the priest asked them to exchange the marriage vows, Mona asked for a moment of silence for Lisa. Then she walked to the pulpit and sang a song dedicated to Lisa's memory. Her gift allowed everyone in the church, who probably were thinking about that day several months ago when Lisa had said goodbye in the video, to feel her presence and feel good about it. Once again it brought Lisa back together with her family and friends in a church. We can think about what that unselfish act did to unify everyone in the church and help the new family have a positive beginning. AND THE GREATEST OF THESE IS LOVE.

"Deeper than the love we take
That we give for loves own sake."
John Greenleaf Whittier

Reflections

1. Can we remember and describe a time on our parenting journey when we reacted to our children's behavior by yelling back at them rather then thinking about what might have caused their negative behavior, pausing, taking a breath and responding?

2. Have we had an experience recently where someone broke into our focused, stressful thoughts and when we reacted to them, they drew back, waited a bit and then asked us questions to find out why we lashed out at them? How did it make us feel? Wasn't it wonderful to be treated so warmly, so unselfishly by the other person?

3. Can we think of times when we misjudged someone's negative behavior at work and made some assumptions about that person without knowing what caused the behavior? Discuss one of these situations with someone.
4. Are there some words we can use to let the other person in our presence know that we really care, that we want to know where they are at and be sensitive to their needs?

CHAPTER 4
GUIDELINE 2
"VALUING EACH PERSON"

If we would learn the secret of building good relations, we would look only for the good in people. And leave the rest to God.

Kenneth H. Mills

Value of Each Person

This guideline assumes that each person is of great value and as such, we should treat each other with dignity, love, respect, sensitivity and caring. We recognize each person as having great value to the organization, family, department, neighborhood business and professional setting. We communicate that value by how we treat them, what we say or don't say to them and what we do or don't do to them. It further assumes the individual, by nature, wants to work hard, be appreciated, be involved, be accepted and feel that they belong.

Feeling Valued is Belonging

The 9-11 attack brought out the best in American behavior. It also brought out the worst. We have read and heard media stories about people who had a certain appearance and certain religious beliefs and ancestry who were mistreated in various ways. Perhaps the day before 9-11 those same people were simply neighbors, friends and fellow workers, and were positively treated. We don't have to look to 9-11 for these negative/positive behaviors as they are exhibited every day across our country and the world. There are thousands of positive and negative stories of how we treat each other in our homes, our communities and our workplaces. These stories dramatically show how much or how little we value each other.

The causes of negative behavior, listed in chapter one, show why we behave toward others in ways that do not value their immense worth. Author and theologian, Dr. John O'Donohue, in his well read book <u>Eternal Echoes—Exploring Our Yearning to Belong</u>, holds the premise that during our entire lifetime, from birth to death, we are yearning to belong. He stated,

> ...to be human is to belong. Belonging is a circle that embraces everything; if we reject it, we damage our nature. The word "belonging" holds together the two fundamental aspects of life: being and longing...belonging is deep...belonging is the heart and warmth of intimacy. When we deny it we grow cold and empty. Our life's journey is the task of refining our belonging so that it may become more true, loving, good and free. We do not have to force belonging. The longing within us always draws us towards belonging and again towards new forms of belonging when we have outgrown the old ones...the most intimate belonging is self-belonging.

The causes of negative behavior may prevent us from feeling this self-belonging for a day, a week or a lifetime. Perhaps it can result in having low self-esteem, not liking and valuing ourselves very much at all. This, of course, can impact how we feel about and value others. Whether it's feeling part of a family, a peer group, a neighborhood, a department, a church, a work place or a customer/patient setting, how we behave may be closely related to the extent to which we feel that we belong, that we are accepted, and that we are welcome. How and what we believe is based on our life's experiences. If our life's experiences have caused us to be a negative or positive person, then we'll tend to assume that we are or are not accepted, that we belong or do not belong to a group. If our life's experiences have given high self-esteem, we tend to feel more comfortable, more at peace, more accepted, than if those experiences resulted in low self-esteem. The more we value ourselves, the more at ease we'll be with groups of people and other potentially high anxiety situations.

Next, we need to value others and exhibit that value by how we treat them, whether they are behaving in a negative or positive way. Of course, it will be much easier if they exhibit positive behavior. We can value others by what we say to them and how we say it, and by what we do or do not do for or to them. I will never forget the first time that I entered the Minnesota Oncology Hematology Center at Abbot/Northwestern Hospital. I was filled with anxiety! I had been diagnosed with cancer by my primary doctor in Mankato, Minnesota. Now I would be meeting with an oncologist to confirm the diagnosis, hear about my expected life span and the chemo treatments. I entered the waiting area with my wife Darlene, walked to the receptionist's desk, gave her (Gloria) my name and said that I had an appointment with Dr. Seng. She gave me a warm smile and said, "while you're waiting to see Dr. Seng would you be willing meet with the business office representative to get that 'stuff' out of the way?" I said yes and sat down to wait. After only a few minutes she said, "He'll be right out, may I get you and Darlene some coffee?" She touched us lightly on the shoulders as she walked away. Keith, the business office person, came out and introduced himself. He invited us to his office. For the first few minutes he engaged us in informal conversation. He told us that our Dr. Seng seemed to be well liked and respected by most everyone. He had ten years of research experience at the University of Minnesota in Non-hodgkins Lymphoma, my kind of cancer. By the time we had filled out the necessary paperwork and were getting up to leave Keith's office, I felt a bit relaxed and "embraced" by the unit.

Both Keith and Gloria helped us feel welcome. We had a feeling of belonging instead of feeling like aliens in a foreign land. We should remember that a feeling of belonging in this kind of situation is no more or less important than belonging in many other situations. Next, I had blood drawn. Even though I was actually the 100th person that day the nurse smiled and welcomed me. I felt more comfortable. Then it was time to meet with Dr. Seng. My name was called and we were escorted to a typical empty waiting room. After a few minutes two nurses entered the room. Each asked for some information from me, but always conversed with us as they did their work. The nurses left and we met with Dr. Seng. From the first handshake to the last words we exchanged he, also, made us feel embraced, that they were there for US. Not one team member from the chemo unit, the catscan department, the medical lab or any other area in between has treated us any differently these past several years.

What did they do beyond what I have already shared?
- Always welcomed us with words and gestures;
- Used our names as soon as they knew them;
- Made eye contact directly and warmly;
- Asked if there was anything they could do;
- Felt bad if we had to wait or if they made a mistake;
- Always apologized if they made a mistake;
- Made us feel like we were never alone from the minute we entered to when we left;
- Always answered our questions or got answers;
- Always thanked us;

- Seemed to care so very much about us and our world;
- Were always so very sensitive to us;
- Helped us feel valued and important; and
- Focused attention so that we felt as though we were the only ones being served!

They touched us deeply, brightening each day that we visited the center. They always made us feel like we belonged to a very special group of people.

Valuing the Individual is Good Business
When we treat employees like we believe that they are important, that they are valued, we create a positive climate for leadership development. This in turn grows our business. This treatment can take many forms from using their names to involving them in decision-making. The following two true stories are dramatic examples of valuing people.

The Glen Taylor Story
The Taylor Corporation, headquartered in Mankato, Minnesota, was founded by Glen Taylor. It is a multi-billion organization that has grown from one to over eighty companies. Glen Taylor is a very modest person but obviously has very special leadership qualities. He has a very strong work ethic and expects the same of his people. There is considerable strong evidence that we could point to as to how Mr. Taylor treats the Corporation's team members. For example, his was one of the first companies to offer childcare for employees. In addition, he built a reputation of trust and integrity. However, one of his strongest traits of specialness relating to valuing the individual is his ability to match people and positions. He has a rich history of learning as much as possible about a potential employee, and when hired, places them in that area/position that best matches their talents, skills and abilities. Also, if individuals were not being successful in one leadership position they were matched with another position that might better suit their strengths.

Treating each person this way gave them a better chance to succeed, made them feel important/valued and gave the Taylor Corporation many excellent leaders who helped build strong successful companies! The Taylor Corporation core values reflect how people are valued: create opportunity and security for employees; respect the potential and significance of every Individual; believe there is always a better way; have a passion for work; and embrace personal, as well as shared responsibility and accountability. So the above is but one of several ways that Taylor Corporation team members FEEL VALUED.

The Dotson Story

The Dotson Company is a very successful foundry located in Mankato, Minnesota. Denny Dotson is the President and CEO of the company. This family-based company has grown at a time when foundries by the hundreds have folded. The reason for its enduring success is its leader, Dennis Dotson. He has several special characteristics but one of the strongest is his belief in and the value of each individual team member. That belief is evident in many areas in the company where individuals' contributions/actions have caused the company to save considerable money, increase productivity, cut costs and increase profits. One fairly recent example of this was the company's announcement to its members that even though business was down no one would be laid off. Instead this would allow the company to get more things done that should have been done in the past when everyone was too busy. Individuals throughout the company have made significant improvements. The results have been astounding, if not surprising. The profits increased even though sales declined. The Dotson Company "walks the talk" as defined in its core values which are: treat people with respect; get individuals involved with the challenges; set high expectations; hold people accountable for their actions; and share the rewards. THE INDIVIDUAL FEELS VALUED!

These stories are about heroes. Our business leaders do not get enough credit for what they do to create jobs, maintain jobs, support communities and grow leaders. The individuals who care about each other and their customers/clients/patients are very special people who make each person feel that they are important, that they belong.

How we treat each other at home, in our neighborhoods and our communities show how much or little we value one another. Each of us has the power to let others know how much they are valued. We can do this by such ways as using names, using eye contact, asking for advice and involving others in decision-making. We can make them feel that they belong in our worlds and in so doing lift them up, brightening their worlds.

"Those who bring sunshine to the lives of others cannot keep it from themselves."

Sir James M. Barrie

Reflections

1. Can we think about a movie we've seen or book we've read which highlights someone valuing others? For example the movies *Radio*, and from years ago *Blackboard Jungle*. What are the themes of these books or movies?
2. Thinking about someone from our past who reached out to us when we were in our teens, what did they do to help us feel important, that we counted, that we belonged?
3. When was the last time that we welcomed a new neighbor, introduced ourselves to a newcomer at church or asked an elderly person if we could carry their groceries or other purchases to the car?
4. Have we ever been in a group where we were the only stranger in the group, didn't know what to say, felt uncomfortable and felt alone? How could someone have helped? What might we do when a new person joins our group?

HUGS CELEBRATE BEING YOU

CHAPTER 5

GUIDELINE 3
"GIVE BACK, GIVE AWAY"

"To excel is to reach your own highest dream. But you must also help others, where and when you can to reach theirs. Personal gain is empty if you do not feel you have positively touched another's life."

Barbara Walters

Stewardship

We each have a <u>stewardship</u> responsibility. It is being of service to each other! This service is about how we treat our family members, friends and neighbors. It also relates to how we treat and serve our co-workers and the people we supervise. Books and articles on effective leaders who follow a steward or servant leadership style have been written for years. Good stewards have special gifts. For example, some of us are natural teachers, some are good writers and others are financial experts. Some are excellent at recognition and celebration. Regardless of our gifts, we can use them to serve others at home, in the community and at work. We each have the power somehow to make a positive difference in the lives of others. Some call it "paying or giving back". Others call it "paying forward". Either way it is the sense that we need to help one another. One motivation for doing this is helping someone who has helped us. Someone gives something to us, or does something for us and we have a strong feeling to return their act of kindness or support. If we give something to the giver, it is called "paying it back." If we can't or choose not to return it to the giver and give to someone else, it is called "paying it forward" or "giving it away."

We all know that these acts make us feel good and really make the world a better place! In order for person-shine or any such approach to encompass or be integrated into an entire department, organization, family, neighborhood or any group, individuals must "spread it" person to person, i.e. one person's action cause another to act...It's called the ripple effect.

Paying It Forward

The first example of stewardship behavior is from a movie called *Pay it Forward*. In the movie, the teacher gives his class an assignment to write a paper about creating something that will change the world for the better. One destitute student devised a plan in which the recipient of a significant act from someone must commit a significant act to three others,who must themselves help three other individuals and so on until the world is changed. In the movie it worked! Good acts are spread from person to person or in essence given away, paying it forward to others.

Hurricane

The second example is a true story as presented in a movie called *Hurricane*. A young man by the name of Hurricane Carter, against all odds became a very successful and famous boxer. However, early in his career, he was mistakenly convicted of murder. He was falsely imprisoned for twenty years. From the beginning, he did everything possible to prove his innocence. Influential friends from time to time would to exert their power to free him. However, because of a corrupt law enforcement officer they were not successful. Hurricane wrote a book telling the story of his innocence, but that too did not help him. A poor young man and his surrogate family were so moved by the book written by Hurricane that they moved from Canada to try to help exonerate him from prison. They did not give up trying until they were successful in freeing him. Hurricane went on to create an association to help falsely accused imprisoned individuals. So far he has helped over twenty-five of them be freed from prison. That is paying it forward!

Give Back, Give Away

Another example is a personal story of a professor that had a major impact on my life. It is about a very successful University of Minnesota Professor, Department Head, Author and President of Foundations, Dr. Richard Ashmun. He encouraged me to return to graduate school and pursue a doctorate. He was a great advisor, always there for me and for all of his students. One of the important lessons that I learned from him was actually a reminder of what my parents had taught me about helping others. In completing my doctorate, I needed to take several courses on campus during the year and over many summer sessions to meet the requirements. I lived in Wisconsin with my wife and family at the time so this meant finding living accommodations. Dr. Ashmun, and his lovely wife Marilyn, graciously allowed me to live in their home for several summers and would even give me food. Each summer I would try to pay him for the food and housing but he would never allow me to give him any money. Finally, it was the last summer and my last day staying at his home. My wife and I agreed on how to try and do it this time. I placed some money in an envelope and as he and I were standing in the driveway saying goodbye, I attempted to place the envelope in his pocket as we hugged. However, he caught my hand, backed away, and almost angrily he said, "Ken, don't you understand? Over the years others have helped me and now I am helping you. Now it's your responsibility to do so for others." I have thought of his comments often and attempted to emulate him in as many ways as possible. We do have the power and the responsibility to brighten others' worlds! We each need to use our unique gifts, our specialness, in giving back, as well as paying forward, to those who have not given to us. We can change the world, One act at a time! One person at a time! One day at a time!

Red Hat Society Celebration

May we feel the power of paying back and paying forward with the power of bringing sunshine to others' worlds over and over again! This is a true story of paying it back. It's a story about three women, Darlene, Jan and Mary, traveling to a forever friend's home who had helped the three travelers in many ways over the years. Now it was her time. It was her turn to enjoy some needed love and support in return. All four women now in their fifties, had been friends for a long time but had not seen each other for a couple of years. Three lived in the Midwest and one in Florida. After a long cold Midwest winter they agreed to fly to Florida for some sunshine, laughter and friendship sharing. Darlene wanted to make it special. Jenny Joseph's famous poem about growing older gracefully, but with individuality and zest, was the inspiration for the creation of the *Red Hat Society*, and gave Darlene an idea. She thought it was exactly what they all needed! Off Darlene went to purchase four red hats and some other gifts. She decorated each hat differently with red feathers, silk flowers, and purple ribbons. She then made four red picture frames to house memory photos of red hat times together. The final gifts were four purple lounging outfits. Darlene flew off to Florida and couldn't wait to give her friends the Red Hat Society outfits! They all loved them! They dressed up in their purple outfits and red hats while Darlene played their favorite song about friendship. They laughed and cried. They wore their outfits all day–had tea, shopped, had dinner overlooking the gulf coast and ended with a sunset cruise while watching the dolphins. Everywhere they went people would come over and ask about the red hats and what they were celebrating. They would comment that they looked like they were having such fun. They named themselves the "Play and Pray Forever Friends Red Hat

Society Chapter." While leaving, they played their song again, and agreed that the words fit them perfectly.

Darlene's story is about many things...It is about paying back and paying forward. Her friends had helped her many times and so often by taking the time to care. She had taken the time and effort to make their introduction into the Red Hat Society a production. The research, gifts, song, performance and naming of their group had been a real celebration for them. She brought rainbows to others' cloudy days and touched others' worlds. Many other people had seen these four happy women in their red hats and purple outfits in the shops and out for dinner. Perhaps they went home to tell their family and friends about what they had seen. And by now how many of them have told others? Maybe they themselves have started their own chapters of the Red Hat Society as a result of this happy occasion! Paying it back, paying it forward!

Let us not forget Sue Ellen, a woman that decided she wanted to make a positive difference for herself and her small group of friends by having a tea party and sharing her idea, which she got from the Jenny Joseph poem. She had a tea party with a few friends. The idea took off and today thousands of women (over fifty) aross the country meet in their Red Hat Society chapters. Just imagine how many thousands of lives it has touched! How many more individuals have found yet a new way to express their love and appreciation for their friends? Paying it forward!

"All people you meet here on earth have something to teach you...there are no random acts...we are all connected...strangers are just family we have yet to come to know."

Mitch Albom

Reflections

1. What are the themes of the movies *Hurricane* and *Pay it Forward* and Mitch Albom's book <u>The Five People You Meet in Heaven</u>?

2. Can we name three people who have done unselfish acts of kindness for us at home, in our community or at work? What were the results? What was accomplished?

3. What are the single greatest acts at home and at work that we have committed to help someone else?

4. Consider if we won 100 million dollars who might be the three or four people outside of family that we would most want to share it with?

Chapter 6
GUIDELINE 4
"TAKE TIME TO CARE"

Share our feelings, express our thoughts, show kindness...care. Extend our happiness, touch someone's heartstrings, cause someone to smile...care. Dare to be positive, offer love to a special person...care.

Kenneth H. Mills

Taking the Time to Care

We have all said or thought more then once, "I'd love to help out, but I'm just too busy right now. I don't have the time! I'm on the way to a meeting, or I just have to get this or that done!" The next time we have a golden opportunity of seeing or hearing someone's call for help and choose whether we respond or not, we and we alone are making the choice. Take the time to care. It'll feel good; we'll like it. To those of us who are saying, "but there are times when I am too busy, how do I know when enough is enough? After all, I am only one person." When each day ends and we look back on it, reviewing the happenings, we and we alone will know if we've done our best and that will be good enough. Real heroes do the best they can and they do it every day!

Mavis Leno (television talk show host, Jay Leno's wife), made an appearance at a conference in Milwaukee, Wisconsin. She

49

spoke on individuals having the power to make a difference and said, "Take one action, no matter how small in whatever grabs your heart. So many do nothing because they feel they don't have control, but that's not true...an Hispanic friend of mine in California says that 'you're not here long, but you are here for good.'"

A Special, Special Olympics

A few years ago at the Annual Special Olympics in Seattle there were nine contestants, all physically or mentally disabled, assembled at the starting line for the hundred-yard dash. At the gun, they all started out, not exactly in a dash, but with a relish to run the race to the finish and win. All, that is, except one little boy who stumbled on the asphalt, tumbled over a couple of times and began to cry. The other eight heard the boy cry. They slowed down and looked over their shoulders. Then they all turned around and went back...every one of them. One girl, with Downs Syndrome, bent down and kissed the fallen boy and said, "this will make it better." Then all nine linked arms and walked together to the finish line. Everyone in the stadium stood, and the cheering went on for several minutes...There possibly wasn't a dry eye in the crowd.

We have such power to make a positive difference in the world, touching others' lives, making their days extraordinary in some way— ONE ACT AT A TIME, ONE PERSON AT A TIME, ONE DAY AT A TIME. It may be responding to someone calling for help, or it may be knowing that someone needs us, and just *showing up* to help out in some way. It may be a simple act of holding a store door open for someone with an armful of packages, letting *the other* car go first, making a call, sending a card, or giving someone a ride. It may be showing up at someone's home to help move to a different house, or helping someone at work with a major project they are having trouble completing. It may be sitting with a friend who just lost someone to cancer.

The City of Angels

About a year and a half ago, my wife Darlene heard that our son and his family were coming to visit us two days earlier and staying a couple days longer then had been originally planned. She got the call about this just after other guests, who had been with us for a couple of days, were leaving. Darlene, took a deep breath, made a list and went to the grocery store—sore back, tired joints and all—to prepare for their coming. She really did want them to come. Then some interesting things happened.

First, as Darlene was going through the checkout lane the lady at the register asked, "How are you?" and "Are you having a bad day?" Darlene told her story. As she left the woman gently touched her arm saying, "I hope that everything goes ok. I'll be thinking of you."

Second, Darlene drove home, was unpacking the groceries, when a flower with a note and the receipt—$1.75—dropped out. The note said "I'll be thinking of you!" signed, Bev. During the weekend Darlene often thought of the wonderful woman and her kind gestures. It made her feel warm, good inside.

Third, after our son left, Darlene bought a special card for Bev, and on several trips to the store looked for Bev to personally show her appreciation. Finally, not finding her, Darlene asked for the manager. He told her that Bev was home recovering from cancer surgery and her husband was recovering from a serious heart attack. Darlene sent the card and they spoke over the telephone. Another day, later on, Darlene stopped for groceries and went home. She unpacked the groceries. Then she realized her purse, with $500 of Christmas money, was missing! She panicked, started to mentally retrace her steps, when she noticed the blinking telephone message. She listened to the message and heard a voice say, "This is Piggly

Wiggly Grocery Store calling. We have your purse. You left it in a cart outside the store and someone turned it in." She got it and found nothing missing.

Fourth, with these two acts in mind Darlene just had to tell her story. She sent a letter to the editor of the local newspaper, celebrating the wonderful people of Sheboygan—CALLING IT A CITY OF ANGELS.

Fifth, after the article was printed Bev called Darlene saying "Thanks so much, I have received so many calls, cards and gifts from the letter to the editor."

Sixth, the pastor of a local church, not ours, used the article for his sermon causing who knows how many other discussions and positive acts.

Seventh, the lady who turned in the purse called Darlene to thank her for writing the letter to the editor. She knew then that Darlene had received her purse and the money. But the lady would not give her name.

Only God knows how many others are telling this story to group after group. And it all began with one person, one day and committing one act...TAKING THE TIME TO CARE!

"When I give, I give myself."

Walt Whitman

Reflections

1. When was the last time someone called us on the phone and asked us for help and we said that we couldn't make it this time? How do we feel about it now?
2. Can we remember a time when one of our children asked us to do something with them and we said no? And another time and we said yes? What's the difference?
3. Is there someone in our lives who just seems to appear

when we need them the most?

4. Think about the time when we helped a friend in a big way! How did we feel afterward? Did our friend show some kind of appreciation?

Recommended Reading

Dr. John O'Donohue's book <u>Eternal Echoes—Exploring Our Yearning to Belong</u> (Cliff Street Books, 1999) has a powerful message on belonging as has been mentioned in an earlier chapter. Presence is one of the ways we can help give people a sense of belonging. On page sixty-three, Dr. O'Donohue describes the power and importance of our presence to others, "...When a friend comes with words of encouragement, a light and lightness visit us and we begin to find the stairs and the door out of the darkness. The sense of encouragement we feel from a friend is not simply her words or gestures; it is rather her presence enfolding and helping us find the concealed door."

CHAPTER 7

GUIDELINE 5
"PLACE PRIORITY ON GIVING
RATHER THAN RECOGNITION"

"No matter what accomplishments you achieve, somebody helped you!"

Althea Gibson

When we Give, Our Heart is Rewarded

"John, we've had the Smiths over so many times. When are they ever going to have us over?"

"I have done so much for the family. Are they ever going to thank me or help me when I need help?"

"I have bought coffee/lunch for my co-workers. Will they ever pay me back?"

"I seem to be doing all the giving in this friendship. When is she going to call me first, write me a note or show interest in my life in some way?"

Do these comments sound familiar? Dr. Phil, noted TV personality and best-selling author, has said on numerous occasions in talking about relationship issues, "you must be getting a payback or you wouldn't continue your behavior; you wouldn't continue a relationship."

Two Very Important Points About Giving and Recognition for Giving

<u>First</u>, *Return action should not be expected* and is described with accompanying stories.

<u>Second</u>, *Priority should not be given on getting recognition for what we've done or given* and is explained with accompanying stories.

First, Return Action Should not be Expected

For healthy relationships and our own self-esteem, we need to recognize that we are getting something by reaching out or we wouldn't be doing it. Remember the well-known saying, "It is better to give than to receive?" Jerry Lewis says during the annual Labor Day MDA Telethon, "Giving is such a selfish act because we always receive more than we ever give." We receive positive feelings and emotional satisfaction knowing that we have helped and have done the right thing—that is a tremendous reward!

This is not to say that we don't want recognition or that we shouldn't recognize others. It is to say that we realize the real reason we reach out is because of the way it makes us feel at the time. We want to do it because of the positive feedback we receive for our acts, because it is our choice and that we are not expecting something in return–we are not expecting others to reciprocate. It is a good idea to be alert to other recognition and acknowledge it when it happens. Although not to the point of keeping score—what I've given versus what I'm getting back from all sources during my lifetime.

The wonderful, fantastic, and emotionally strong characteristic of this guideline is that there is a guarantee that comes with it. *The guarantee is that when we need the recognition the most and expect it the least it will come, and when it comes, it will be in the most powerful and amazing ways!*

I make a statement when I am giving seminars that some of the audience will be sending me letters, or calling me in the next few weeks, sharing their own experiences. They tell me they were amazed that someone contacted them in some positive powerful way, letting them know how much they were valued. These comments are usually unexpected, coming from someone we least thought would be appreciative of their actions. Furthermore, they usually received this recognition at a time in their lives when they needed it the most.

Darlene and Ken's Friendship Lesson

My wife, Darlene, and I suffered some very bad times. Within a three year period we lost our life savings, our home was destroyed by water, our careers were severely damaged and our health was seriously affected. As part of a scheme to fire our institution's president, I was attacked with negative media for more than two years and was eventually fired. During those three years, from time to time, we found ourselves saying how disappointed we were that this or that individual or couple had not called or in some way remembered us by offering emotional or physical support. In every instance, only a few days or weeks after mentioning them, one or more of those same people would contact us, with cards, telephone calls, gifts or by stopping in just to give us their support. Most often it would happen *when we needed it the most and expected it the least*. We need to remember, if someone has not reciprocated, perhaps we have not needed it the most.

Irish Eyes are Smiling

Mr. Ted Smith, a retired Irish fireman, was given a fireman's hero funeral upon his death. At the gravesite with firemen standing at attention, they gave their final salute—their large silver bell rang twenty-five times celebrating his twenty-five years of service. But for Darlene and me, he was a hero for a different reason. Ted Smith had brightened so many worlds for so long and taught others how to do the same by what he said, how he treated others, and how he lived and worked. Darlene and I had lived next door to Ted and his wife Val for four years. They were the perfect neighbors. Ted and Val let Darlene use their washer/dryer because we didn't have one. Darlene and I didn't have room for guests to sleep over and inevitably they ended up sleeping at Ted and Val's. Eventually, Darlene and I bought a house and moved to our first home across town which greatly our reduced contact with Ted and Val. Then the bottom fell out and we suffered the bad times mentioned above. We had three very difficult years during which I lost my job and our life savings. Just when we thought no one cared enough to support us! Just when we least expected someone to stand up and speak out for us and give us support! Just when we needed it the most! A most overwhelming event took place, brightening our lives in a way that was beyond description!

Part of my job required me to be at a community forum where our board was inviting community input on our college's offerings. I arrived early; 400 people filled the room. I began to notice many people whom I knew and who wouldn't normally be at this kind of event. The Board chairperson opened the meeting by inviting input on the college's offerings. A lifelong friend and organizer of the support group for me strode to the podium and said, "My name is John Bailey. My wife, Sherry, and I are friends with Ken and Darlene. We want to know what is happening here." Then our Pastor and forever friend, Father John Murphy spoke firmly in the same way and then another and another, and another. I soon realized that most of the people in the group were not there to give the board input on the college's offerings but to support me. The next day's new media carried the whole positive evening. From that night on I no longer felt the negative eyes of the community on me. Instead I felt strong support. Ted and Val Smith were a part of that throng of friends who helped to organize it. That night many years ago we learned all about defining friendships, about *brightening others worlds when they least expect it and when it's needed the most!*

Second, Our Priority Should not be on Getting for What We've Given or Done

This part is about putting others first in giving recognition (credit) for ideas, decisions and accomplishments. Our light won't stay hidden under a "bushel basket." This does not mean that we do not want recognition. It does not mean that we will not receive recognition. It does mean that if we spend a lot of time thinking about all the great things that we've done and how we should be receiving recognition for them, those expectations might not be fulfilled. If we've done good things, if we've made contributions, we'll most often receive credit in due time, perhaps just when we need it the most. We need to remember how good it feels to have someone talk positively to us, and to others, about our contributions. We should make a practice of doing the same for others, helping their star to shine, brightening their worlds!

Wisdom tells us that as we get older if we're secure within ourselves the more that we try to give credit to others, the more it will come back to us. Everyone wants and needs credit/recognition for doing good things. The potentially harmful part is when we want it too much, pursue it too much or think about it too much. One of the best ways to keep this from happening is to practice giving credit to others as often as possible. Sometimes, we may have to overcome the strong desire to seek credit for something and give it to someone else.

Giving Credit Away

"No man is an island" is a very well known saying. It speaks to many things such as whenever we're in need there is always someone who can help us, if we're open to that help. Or it reminds us of our humility. Whenever we're about to take bows for some super deed done, award received, act performed, or speech given, we need to remember who and what made it possible for us to excel in some special way to allow us to be receiving the recognition. However, in order to do that we must be secure within ourselves. In doing so we put aside our pride and ego and give others the credit.

Ways to Practice Giving Credit
There are many behaviors we can practice to focus on our giving credit to others. The following list comes from working with business and industry, interviews with seminar participants and observing human behavior:
- **give credit when credit is due.**
- **anonymously convey positive actions towards others (very powerful).**
- **sit in the rear of the room—then you may be invited to the front.**
- **develop and use our special gifts, acknowledging those who have invested in us.**
- **give praise often, even for the little things.**
- **be our own best friend, feeling good about what we do.**
- **support others when difficult decisions are to be made.**
- **do informal mentoring without wanting rewards/ recognition.**
- **seek humility in all things.**
- **internalize, feel the strength, joy and immense satisfaction from accomplishing goals, instead of getting recognition.**

Ask an author, a poet, a composer or a musician to tell us when they feel their greatest sense of accomplishment, their highest highs. They'll probably tell us the *first time* is when they complete their work, be it painting, book, song or poem. The *second time*, is when someone they respect reads, views or hears it and shows strong positive signs of being moved by it. The *third*, is when a greater audience responds positively to it, and *the last time* is when they receive some award/reward for it.

A Story about Recognition
Tuesdays With Morrie is a true story and was a best seller for many months. It became a wonderful movie, starring Jack

Lemon. This story is a great lesson for us, on giving others credit for our contributions, our accomplishments and our successes in life. The whole story became public in print and movie because the author becomes aware, from the media, that one of his college professors of many years ago, Morrie, was dying. He decides to visit the gentleman in his home and express his appreciation for the impact he had on his life. By the end of the first visit, Morrie invited him back. He went again and again and again every Tuesday until Morrie died. He went back because he was learning about life from this dear old man. The moral of the story for us is that he tried to give credit/recognition to someone else and in the end received more than he could ever have given or dreamed from that one visit. Meeting with Morrie gave him strong emotional support, a very successful book and a movie, and a huge career boost beyond his wildest imagination. Selfishly speaking, the more that we try to give credit away, if honestly done, the more it will come back to us in rich rewarding ways! What a blessing! But in order to do this successfully, we may have to work at putting ego and pride aside in order not to fill our minds/feelings with negative selfishness. Thoughts like, "I deserved that award/ reward more then they did," come into our minds. It's human to do so, and that is why it's so important to *place no priority on receiving credit/recognition.*

Receiving Due Credit in Due Time

We know when we commit an unselfish act of giving a word or a deed, our first reward is the feeling inside our hearts that we have helped someone in some way. And in so doing we may never be famous but we will be great whether we want to or not. Great in the eyes of the sunshine recipients and in the feelings in our hearts and in the minds of those who know us. Very often as our story is told, it is valued by those in our neighborhood, our community, our region, perhaps in our country and even around the world. Some examples are the pastor in the Senior Orphans story, the student in <u>Tuesdays With Morrie</u> and the following story about my father-in-law, Ted Hanson!

Ted Hanson committed many unselfish acts in his life. One of the most unselfish and touching was his commitment to a unique Catholic Knights of Columbus program which gave support to those who died alone or with few people around them. Ted was the volunteer leader for this effort in his hometown for years. It was something that few people wanted to volunteer for. The media, funeral homes, hospitals and other churches in town were aware of this program. When someone was dying alone, Ted would get a call. He would then make calls until he got enough volunteers to sit with the dying person. After they died, Ted would make the funeral arrangements and the same team would be present at the wake and the funeral, which were very simple ceremonies. No one in that town ever had to die or be buried alone. We found out later that quite often Ted would not be able to get any volunteers. He would be the lone company for the lonely and the forgotten at the funeral home, the church and the grave. Many Friday and Saturday nights Ted would leave a celebration of some kind, or forego a night out after a hard week's work, to "sit with the lonely!" Did others appreciate it, or even realize it? Yes! They turned out in large numbers for Ted's funeral twenty plus years ago. The church was full, packed, with many people standing. The Knights of Columbus, dressed in full regalia, lined the aisle honoring Ted for his unselfish acts and recognizing the hundreds of hours he sacrificed for the lonely and the forgotten. Darlene, his daughter, said that "During those years when I watched my dad leave home to carry out his mission, I wondered how anyone could possibly be left alone. Now, after thirty-eight years of being a registered nurse in nursing homes and hospitals, and observing many instances when people are truly alone, I understand why he did this and what a hero he was!"

In the stories about the Pastor and the Senior Orphans program, the writer in <u>Tuesdays With Morrie</u> and Ted Hanson being with the lonely, we learn about what their acts did for others. We know for certain that they made a significant positive difference in the lives of many people.

These individuals were great because of what they did. All of them were miracle makers, and although they didn't ask for it, they became famous in and beyond their circles of influence. In Ted's case his fame actually grew after his death when the filled church heard of his many acts of touching the lonely and the forgotten. The pastor's story has only begun! It is anticipated that the Senior Orphans' program will grow and flourish regionally and nationally.

"It is man's duty to awaken the understanding of the inner self and to know his own real inner greatness. Once he knows his true worth, he can know the worth of others."

Swami Muktananda

<u>Reflections</u>

1. Remember a time when someone received some kind of recognition we should have received. How did it makes us feel? Did we do anything about the injustice?
2. Have we ever received credit for something positive that we didn't do or say? How did we respond?
3. Was there a time that after giving someone a large gift and not receiving even a thank you for it, we felt hurt or upset? How did we deal with it without it destroying a relationship?
4. Think of an instance where we worked hard to complete a difficult project at work that no one else could do? How did we feel about completing before anyone else knew it was done? How did we feel when co-workers congratulated us? How did we feel when our supervisor publicly complimented us?

5. Is there someone at our workplace who never seems to buy coffee or share supplies? How does that make us feel?
6. Have we ever shoveled the driveway or cut the lawn for a neighbor? Even before they thanked us? How did doing it make us feel?
7. Does this guideline seem to relate to part of the movie *It's A Wonderful Life* with Jimmy Stewart or Mitch Albom's book <u>Tuesdays With Morrie</u>?

<u>Recommended Readings</u>

Don Miguel Ruiz, author of the best seller, <u>The Four Agreements</u>, wrote about this topic in another way in his book, <u>The Mastery of Love</u>. His point is that we must love ourselves first before we can love others. We must also accept others the way they are. He states, "With these three points, the truth, forgiveness and self-love, the whole world will heal.... Imagine, if all humans could start being more truthful with themselves, start forgiving everyone and start loving everyone."

CHAPTER 8
GUIDELINE 6
"LISTEN TO OTHERS' WORDS
AND FEELINGS"

"A little girl lost a playmate in death and one day reported to her family that she had gone to comfort the sorrowing mother. 'What did you say?' asked her father. 'Nothing.' she replied. 'I just climbed up on her lap and cried with her.'"

Charles Swindoll

Guideline Eight Meaning
This guideline is another very important part of Person-Shine. It means that we listen to the meaning of what someone else is saying. We should be interested and care about what our partners, family, friends, co-workers, supervisors and neighbors are saying to us through their words and actions. We can demonstrate this interest in several ways. However, listening to what they have to say is one of the best ways. It is important that others view us as easy to talk with, open to two-way discussion, not telling everyone what we hear from others and sincerely wanting to hear what they have to say.

"The duty of love is to listen"

Paul Tillich.

This true story could be about the couple across the street, down the block or across town, as the content has happened or is happening in relationships everywhere. It frames out the meaning of this guideline perfectly.

Listening to our Partners
Ann and Bill had been married about fifteen years when the realization hit Bill that he hadn't been listening to his wife. Prior to this awakening Bill had played out the role he thought his father had played. This included "allowing" his wife to work outside the home, as long as she worked the night shift, did all of the housework and they used the money she made for him to attend graduate school. Bill, being the provider, justified his working long hours and traveling out of town for work because that was his role. Bill didn't change diapers, didn't help with the household duties and decided when and how he would listen to Ann. Bill was a traditional chauvinist of the times. *This was about to change!*

On a brisk fall morning Bill drove to a company training session. Little did he know, this would be the day that he and Ann started on a road to significant behavioral changes. It probably saved their marriage and most certainly brought more happiness to them as a couple. The speaker of the day was of the "I'm Ok, Your Ok" movement of the 70's. She asked the 200 people in the audience to role play several of her major topics with the person next to them, regarding the child and adult within each of them. Finally she said, "Assume you are your mother talking about you." Bill spoke to his partner as his mother, describing how she loved him and what kind of son he had been. Somewhere during the conversation a light came on in Bill's mind and he thought, "I've got to get home, as soon as possible, and talk with Ann." Bill drove home very fast. He saw Ann's car in the driveway and felt a sense of relief that she wasn't working that day. He walked into their house yelling, "Ann, are you home?" She was there! He approached her saying, "Ann, do I decide when I am going to let you talk and when I am going to listen to you?" Ann quietly responded, "Yes you do Bill!" He asked, "Why haven't you told me?" She said, "I've been trying to for many years." Bill didn't change his behavior completely. However, on that day he made a commitment to Ann that he try more often to be there for her, listen to her and put her feelings first.

Bill kept trying and Ann took assertiveness training classes to learn how to better express her feelings. Then Bill enrolled in a psychology class. The professor asked the students to keep journals. Each week they handed them in to the professor. He would read them, comment on them and return them at the next session. He noted on one of Bill's papers, "Bill, you write a lot about family and your family's daily activities, about how much you love your three children and wife. You also mention that you have family discussions. Please make a tape of one of the discussions and share it with me." Bill had an idea. His parents were coming from out of town to visit that weekend so Bill would ask his mom and dad if he could tape them during the dinner discussion. They agreed. The first night of the visit there was a lively two-hour discussion. The next class session Bill turned in the tape. Two weeks later Bill got home from work early, picked up the day's mail and noticed a package from his professor. He hurriedly opened it and read the three pages of comments the professor had written about the taped discussion. However, Bill focused on the last few sentences. The professor wrote, "Bill, it was a wonderful evening. Almost everyone except your wife asked questions, shared experiences and had a great time listening to each other. The only one listening to her was your six-year-old son." Bill quickly played the tape. It seemed everyone, except Ann, was having fun. Every once in a while she would to try speak, ask someone a question or share a story. The most response she got was a grunt from someone. However her six-year-old son would say, "What mommy, What did you say mommy?" Bill had tears in his eyes and realized that he still had a long way to go on his journey of positive behavior change to treating his wife as a full partner. He really needed to listen to her words and feelings. The *outcome*? Their marriage has survived. They are successful because a deep and powerful love is the base of their relationship. That love helped Bill and Ann as they worked their way through the stormy times. They are much better at honoring one another…sharing their presence, focusing on the person, listening to words and feelings.

" '*And what is as important as knowledge?' asked the mind. 'Caring, [hearing,] and seeing with the heart,' answered the soul.*"

Author unknown

Brightening the World of our Loved Ones
"*The most exquisite pleasure is giving pleasure to others!*"

Jean De La Bruyere

The focus of this message is on the most important people in our worlds—our loved ones. Why? Because these are the people who should know us the best. They should be the most able to accept us for who and what we are, love us for our strengths and help us manage our weaknesses. They should be the people we most want to be with during our happy times and our sad times, with who we want to pray, celebrate, laugh and cry. These are the people with whom we'll be spending most of our lives. Quite often when asked who is our best friend, we'll name our loved ones. If that's true, then isn't it also true that we should do everything in our power to please, celebrate, satisfy, accept, love, support, listen to and help them grow. We try to give them mental sunshine to brighten their world in every way possible!

Have we? Do we? Can we? Most of us would probably say that we could do better. We could be more committed to giving those special people more sunshine in their lives. If that is the case, let's look at some things we could do to improve. In readings, interviewing people and listening to seminar participants I have learned at least some of the reasons we don't brighten each others' worlds the way we should:

- **We put our best faces on for the rest of the world and our worst for our loved ones. The saying, "you always hurt the one you love the most," seems to be true, at least some of the time.**
- **We simply don't talk/listen to each other.**
- **We focus on the negative...the weaknesses...in the other person, rather than the positives...the strengths.**
- **We don't celebrate enough...holidays, birthdays, happenings, accomplishments, blessings and just being.**
- **We allow the anger, the feelings of insecurity, the sadness, the stresses, and the worries within us to become obstacles to a relationship with our loved ones...even though they are not the cause for these feelings. We lash out at them, bringing dark clouds instead of sunshine into their worlds.**
- **We allow a desire to change, to improve, to do away with the weaknesses in our loved ones to grow...even though we know that the same behaviors may have been the reasons we fell in love with them.**

Can We, Do We, Want to Change?

So what are we going to do about our lax behavior towards those that we love the most? If we want to change that behavior, really want to change it, then we need to consciously work at it. Here are a few helpful hints:

- **Create some thinking/meditation time just for us. It might be driving home from work, staying up late,** sitting alone in some quiet surroundings, to focus our thinking on our partner...remembering the first time we told them how much we loved them, the first dates, happy times together and special sharing moments. Make a list of our partner's positive traits, then write a love note to them telling them how special they are and why we love them. Do this at least once a week.

- Do random acts of lovebuilding. For example, call from work and invite them to lunch. Pick them up at noon to go to a surprise location. Have no special topic for lunch. Our responsibility will be to listen, to ask questions, to respond openly to questions, always giving our total presence.

- Tell our partner daily, "I LOVE YOU," when parting for work, travel or any reason.

- Make certain to offer physical hugs at least twice a day.

- Spend some time, at least once or twice a week, just quietly sitting close together, listening to music, or watching a special TV show.

- Ask our partner if they would agree to a date night once a week. Take turns being host and the guest, and have the date locations and agendas be surprises!

There are many more actions that we could list. We might begin with one and hopefully add more of the above actions to brighten our loved one's world, which in turn, will make us feel better and eventually improve our relationship. The power we have to create sunshine relationships is immense! It should be added that the cost for most of the above is only our time. Imagine the mighty return for the minor investment! We know that it will take time, commitment and a real effort. We'll be doing some or all of the above, sometimes when we really don't feel like doing them at all. Those are very likely the best times to do them as our relationships may need them the most at those times.

May we walk arm in arm, heart to heart into the sunshine and know that we have captured the most joy for each other out of each moment!

Kenneth H. Mills

Reflections

1. How do we give our loved ones our *presence?*
2. Reading Dr. John O'Donohue's book, <u>Eternal Echoes</u> (pps. 59-62) about *presence* and viewing the Reality TV show *The Apprentice*, how much do the show contenders give their presence by listening to others' words and feelings?
3. Can we remember a time at work when a colleague told us they were dissatisfied with their job and we never really listened to their pain and frustration?
4. Can we think of a time when one of our children (no matter the age) attempted to break through our wall of concentration to ask or tell us something and we never really gave them our presence?

CHAPTER 9
GUIDELINE 7
"ONLY ASK IF YOU'RE GOING TO LISTEN"

"The relationship between music and life is not only that of one language to another; it is also the relationship of the perfect world of listening to the whole world of seeing."

Nietzsche

Asking the Second Question

One way to help others is by asking, and asking, and asking–about the people around us–and all the time listening with our ears, minds, and hearts. We greet people we know by saying, "Hi, how are you?" and the reaction we inevitably hear is "Fine" or "Ok!" However, we should remember to make certain that we have their attention by holding their hand a little longer, making eye contact, or moving a little closer to the person and asking the second question, "I really want to know. How are you?" After the second question, we will almost always get a better response, one that begins to tell us how the person really feels.

We have come to expect greetings as a habit so therefore, do not usually respond with anything significant when someone asks us how we are. We don't expect that people want to hear

71

how we really are. It comes as a surprise when the person really does want to listen to us! Remember, it is extremely important to keep the focus on the person, to continue to really listen after asking someone how he or she really is.

The process of asking questions and carefully listening helps to build trust and relationships over a period of time. It is even more important in long-term relationships to use this approach, such as with spouses, friends, and fellow workers. We should not take them for granted. Once, during a seminar I was leading, I sat in on a small group discussion. The group was discussing the topic, "how to improve our love relationship." One man commented that his love partner wanted him to share more of his deep feelings and concerns about his work. He felt that she was not committing the time and effort that he needed to open up.

Mike Did Ask the Second Question

If we ask someone a question, they should believe that we are sincere, wanting to know their thoughts and feelings. Otherwise they probably won't give us their true and complete response. Another small group participant shared a personal experience. Mike was returning to his office from a meeting downtown. He was in a hurry to make his next meeting. Upon entering a hallway in the building he met a colleague he supervised. Mike said, "Hi, Hank, How are you?" and rushed past. Hank responded, "Ok," but as Mike hurried past him he noticed something in Hank's eyes that bothered him. Mike stopped, turned and said, " No, Hank, really, how are you?" Hank stopped, turned and walked towards Mike with tears streaming down his face! "I'm not doing so well today, Mike." Mike asked him to come to his office, closed the door, rescheduled his appointment and talked to Hank. He found out that Hank's son had attempted suicide and did not want to talk to his parents. Hank really needed to talk to a friend who would really care about him and would listen to him.

Did Mike save Hank's emotional life? Maybe not, but on that day, at that moment Hank needed to share his situation, his feelings with someone. Mike gave him his total presence. *Mike had asked Hank the second question, and really listened to Hank's response.* Hank may never forget that day.

Taking the Time to Listen

Another small group participant shared her story. She was in a department meeting at the end of the day and asked a colleague, "How are you doing?" Even though she asked her colleague she did not take the time to listen. She was in a hurry to get home to her family so her husband could go to a meeting. However, her colleague responded, "Things could be better." This touched her mind and her heart. She responded, "What do you mean?" She learned that her colleague's husband had just been diagnosed with cancer and would not talk about it. They talked about it and she even volunteered to go to the woman's house to talk with her husband. The colleague said, "No, but thank you for the offer." The woman went home, confronted her husband, getting him to talk about his feelings and their relationship improved. Her colleague asked the *second question, then listened.*

Both of these stories are about individuals who took the time to listen to others–who took the time to ask the second question, really listened and cared about how another person truly felt. Remember–*Only ask if you're going to listen!*

Companies Need to Improve

Quality experts over the past twenty some years have been telling management to seek their employees' input. Dr. Edward Deming, "father" of the Quality Process, began taking management to task on really listening to their employees. He strongly encouraged them to implement the Quality Process, using employee teams to improve systems and operations. However, he cautioned them to *really listen and consider* team members recommendations—teams don't need all of their input used, but they need to know that it was considered. Many companies, taking Dr. Deming's advice, became very successful at improving their organization's bottom line and their employee's morale.

Literally, hundreds of company executives have taken the necessary time to move down the quality road. However, many of them failed, in part because they asked their employees' for input, received it, but then ignored it. This destroyed the trust that they had built up with their employees over time.

A leader, who use to be with IBM, recently said to me, "Some companies miss the boat with their investment in training. I know several stories of companies sending employees to excellent training, and then, when they return excited to implement what they have learned, they are discouraged, even defeated, by business roadblocks…perhaps procedures don't accommodate the new idea, or software is necessary that can't be ready for months. This is a variation of *only ask if you're going to listen*…don't stimulate new thinking if you are not going to consider new ideas. Of course, the best companies will turn this guideline inside out to both stimulate and consider employee's new ideas."

Parents' Behavior Show their Children They are Listening

How can we be better parents? First we know that we are parents forever! The joy and anxiety of that miracle is called new life. It comes into our lives as parents and hits us with such emotional blasts, raising many questions and fears. We all know that parenting is a 24/7 responsibility that requires excellent listening skills. The following are guidelines for becoming better parents. Each one assumes a foundation of listening to our children:

1. First, from birth to death every person throughout their entire lives yearns to belong. We, as parents, need to exhibit

every behavior that lets our children know that they belong to us, to our whole family, to the neighborhood, to the community. These behaviors include showing them that we love them in every way possible, by saying it, hugging them, celebrating them, asking them for their opinions and suggestions, giving them our presence and in other ways showing them they are a part of us and important to us and the entire family.

2. Truly listen to their questions, their comments, their concerns, and considering their body language and feelings.

3. Give them structure by setting boundaries with their input, as they get older–in all parts of their lives.

4. It is important as parents to not undermine each other when dealing with our children's behavior. It is also very important that both parents never "gang-up" on them.

5. Teach children how to make decisions and exercise good judgment. This can help them grow and mature, feel good about themselves and gain confidence.

6. Be consistent, provide stability in the home.

7. Celebrate our children's existence every chance that we get in every way possible–birthdays, achievements, exhibiting positive behaviors, special events or no reason other than their being in our lives. When celebrating we make them feel special, important, loved, deeply valued by us, which makes their lives shine–makes them feel accepted and "ten feet tall."

Practicing these seven guidelines with our children will help them brighten their worlds–giving them mental sunshine each and every day!

"The best executive is the one who has sense enough to pick good men [and women] to do what he wants done, and self-restraint enough to keep from meddling with them while they do it." [i.e. Ask for input, listen to it, consider it, respond to it and recognize the people who gave it.]

Theodore Roosevelt

75

Reflections

1. Are we like the people in our lives who ask us how we are and before we can answer begin telling us something about their life? How or how not?
2. Do we usually ask the second question after asking someone, "how are you?" Explain.
3. Can we remember a work situation where the supervisor asked for input on a decision and then didn't acknowledge it (I didn't say use the input, just acknowledge it)? How did we feel about it?
4. How can we include our children or love partner when making decisions that impact their lives?

Recommended Reading

1. <u>Zapp!</u>, a book by William C. Byham tells us that we can be successful in empowering others by listening and responding with empathy as long as we care deeply and want to hear what the other person has to say.
2. In Don Miguel's best selling book, <u>The Four Agreements</u>, he shares that in any situation, "we should not make assumptions. Find the courage to ask questions and to express what you really want. Communicate with others as clearly as you can go avoid misunderstandings, sadness and drama."

CHAPTER 10

GUIDELINE 8
"SAY YOU'RE WRONG, SAY YOU'RE SORRY"

I've often been fascinated with Robert Bly's golden bees and their ability to fashion "from old, bitter sorrows, / white honeycomb and sweet honey."

Kenneth H. Mills

Saying We are Wrong, Saying We are Sorry

Have we ever been wrong? Have we ever made a wrong decision and admitted it? Have we ever been the first to admit that we were wrong in an argument? How did we feel? It may not have bothered us at first. The goal is to be sensitive about wrong behavior, admit it and improve by exhibiting good behavior. If we make a point of practicing admitting that we are wrong, it may become a positive habit that will help relationship building.

The next giant step is to be able to say, "we're sorry" or some other words of apology. A secure, stable person can use these words rather easily because they do not take that action as an admission of weakness, but as a simple yet important act. We

77

tell someone that "we made a mistake and we respect and care about you, therefore, we apologize." It tells the other person(s) that we know that we are human and that we can and will make mistakes.

Responding to an Apology and Admission of Being Wrong

How should we respond if the other person in a relationship is the first to say they are sorry or they are wrong? We need to recognize that it may not have been easy for them to make those admissions and with words and actions show our appreciation. We need to acknowledge that this is positive behavior and in some way reward it. For example, <u>In Search of Excellence</u> expert Tom Peters believes that we should "celebrate that which we want more of." Therefore if our responses to these admissions are positive, it may make it easier for the person to continue the behavior.

Imagine a World

- Imagine a world where after being in bitter arguments everyone admits that they were wrong.
- Imagine a world where presidents, CEO's, community leaders and politicians readily admit mistakes and say they are wrong.
- Imagine a world where medical doctors admit a mistake or that they're wrong and someone was hurt or died as a result of it! And if they had done so over the years would there be fewer law suits, hence lower insurance costs to the patient?
- Imagine a world where politicians would say that they voted for "X" bill, but they were wrong or that they made a mistake!
- Imagine a world where presidents/CEO's say that they were wrong or made mistakes, rather then blaming others! For example, how many management people connected with stock scandals said that they were wrong or made a mistake, or even that they were sorry?

78

Such a world may never exist, but we can hope for the better and do our part to improve it. We shouldn't be too hard on the authority people of the world. Many of us have the same problem. However the problem is magnified when the behavior of those in authority affects a larger community of so many others. If it's our world of one on one relationships, the people impacted may be hurt and that's terrible for them, but at least the harm is limited to those closest to us at that time.

Why is it so difficult to imagine such a world? Why don't some pillars of society say that they're wrong, made a mistake or are sorry? Is it because of fear, of being sued, that people will think less of them or loss of pride? Why do some people in powerful positions seem to have problems with it? Would it be better for them to risk the embarrassment of admitting mistakes and do it?

However, it's far easier to tell someone else to do it then do it ourselves. Those who can practice this behavior usually gain the respect of those around them. They will find out that there is great power in saying and meaning the words, " I'm sorry, I made a mistake, I'm wrong." It lets people know that we're human, we're vulnerable. It often disarms our critics and certainly may make our supporters feel worthy of their support...and thankful and proud of us.

The Oncologist Who "Gets It"
There are many physicians and professionals in all areas who are exhibiting humble behavior by taking responsibility for problems, mistakes and inappropriate conduct. One such example is Dr. John Seng, and his team, at Minnesota Oncology in Minneapolis, Minnesota. In Chapter four I shared the story, of how over the past five plus years the entire team helped my wife and me feel welcomed, embraced. During one of our visits a professional in the chemo unit did not give me the complete set of drugs. I missed getting one

bag. At the beginning of the second of a three-day session, while in the waiting room at the chemo unit, I was informed that Dr. Seng wanted to see me immediately. I entered the small room and Dr. Seng came, sat down and with a very serious face told me an error had been made in administering my chemo drugs the day before.

First, Dr. Seng apologized for the error. Next, he gave me the options necessary to rectify the error, which included opening the office on Saturday just for me. We decided on the best option, which was to complete the remaining procedure and not take the missed drug. Then he told me that the nurse who had made the error, had spent the previous evening calling hotels and restaurants trying to find me. I asked him if she would be disciplined for the error because I did not want her to be reprimanded in any way. He said, "No, except for noting it in the records." I thanked him for being open and honest with me and apologizing for the mistake. I also asked if I could have that nurse give me the chemo drugs that morning because I felt that she probably was stressed out and I wanted to put her at ease. She came to me crying and saying how sorry she was for making the error. We hugged, we all cried, and she gave me the drugs. IN THIS STORY IT WAS SO EASY FOR US TO ACCEPT THEIR APOLOGY AND FEEL GOOD ABOUT THE ENTIRE INCIDENT BECAUSE OF THEIR HONEST BEHAVIOR. Did they have a choice? Yes, they had a choice in how and what they would tell me. We have told this story as a positive, instead of a negative one, to many people who quite often want to tell their negative experiences where professionals were not open and apologetic.

Deming's Message to Presidents/CEO's

Dr. Deming, world wide quality movement leader, for years told those in management that they needed to be accountable for the mistakes made, bad systems used and the poor performance of employees. Leaders have the power to put the processes and systems in place to make the best decisions possible. They have the power to seek input from their employees in order to make the best decisions. Therefore, they should admit their mistakes, get their employees involved and make better decisions. However, it is quite difficult to do. Otherwise why would leaders like Tom Peters, author of <u>In Search of Excellence</u> and management expert, be able to make millions of dollars by researching highly successful organizations in which leaders put their customers and employees first by listening to them and involving them in the decision-making process? The leaders of those organizations know that by giving some of the power away they gain much power in return. This holds true for those same leaders in saying they're wrong, sorry or made a mistake.

A President Learns a Lesson

John, President of a middle sized organization in the Midwest, tells his story about learning a lesson from saying he was wrong, sorry for his mistake and apologizing, and in so doing really gaining power and success for the organization and himself.

> "I was President in a new organization which had been created from two rather old institutions. The finance executive took a medical leave, eventually quitting, taking critical information about the finances with him, in his head. I appointed an interim— non-finance—person from within the organization to lead the finance area. This was a bad decision. The organization got into great financial difficulty, lost reserves, had payroll problems effecting about sixty percent of the employees, along with other related issues. Finally, I hired a well experienced, degreed, talented finance person. He turned the place around in a matter of two years. However, in the middle of the worst of times,

right after he was hired, the employees strong union leadership presented me with a written statement and a list of questions about the status of their institution. They suggested that I attend a meeting of their members that was taking place in a few minutes. I entered the room and found the majority of the members looking very upset. They had a right to feel that way. I said that I had read their paper and would respond in writing as soon as possible. However, I wanted to hear what they had to say today. After everyone had been heard I said the most important words that I could have said at that time.

First, I want to tell you that I take full responsibility for the financial mess that we are in and I apologize to the individuals that I placed in the interim position. *Second*, I apologize to all the staff for the spot that I have placed us in. *Third*, you said today, and in your paper, that you love this place and are hurt because of my mistakes and have lost confidence in me. You want to know that I'm going to do my part, as president, to restore the positive image of this organization. The new finance person with all of our support, has the background, experience and ability to help solve our problems. *Fourth*, I too love this place and am working night and day, and will continue to do so, to have us be proud and feel good about its image and operations. BUT IF YOUR MEMBERSHIP, AT ANY TIME, WANTS MY CONTRACT, WANTS ME TO LEAVE, ALL THAT YOU HAVE TO DO IS TO ASK FOR IT THROUGH YOUR LEADERSHIP.' The union leadership did not

ask for my resignation and from that day, the
membership and I grew closer and stronger
with more and more respect for one another.
The organization became a leader in its field
winning financial awards every year."

One on One Relationships

So what about our one on one relationships in our everyday
lives? Do we say that we are sorry, that we have made mistakes
and that we're wrong to those close to us? I believe that most,
if not all of us, want to do this. I recently discussed this with
some seminar participants who said that they believe the
majority of people generally would rate between one to four
on a scale of ten, with one being those people who would
most often be the first to say they're sorry. They believe that
the majority would behave this way most of the time because
they are comfortable with themselves, care about those
around them and want to be supportive. However, in the
discussions they also said that they believed the times people
do not behave this way, who do not admit they are wrong, is
because of ego and pride. They may not be secure within
themselves. They many not love themselves first.

I also asked those in the seminar discussions who rated
themselves from one to four, "what do you do to be able to
behave this way i.e. admitting mistakes, saying you are wrong
or that you are sorry?" They said:
(1) We look at our hearts.
(2) Do we really care about the other person?
(3) Do we need and want them in our lives?
(4) Are we sensitive to the hurts, fears and happenings in
their lives?
(5) Can we sacrifice our own ego and pride or the need to be
right? Or do we internalize the hurt knowing that we need
them and want them in our lives?
(6) How often are we the first to say, "I'm sorry" or "I'm
wrong?"

The discussion also brought out two other very significant points. First, the older we get the easier it becomes for most people to use those words. This may be because pride becomes less and less important as we experience life's challenges and hurts. Second, from time to time, we find ourselves thinking about those times when we wished that we had behaved better, perhaps swallowing pride and hurt, in deference to those that we loved and cared about.

Research
Finally, the discussion and other research clearly show us that it is very powerful to say that "I'm sorry," "I'm wrong," or "I made mistakes." It disarms the other person(s). It gives us a sense of peace as we deal with our pride and ego. It means that we are more secure within ourselves and don't have to always win. A major factor is that we can learn so much from our mistakes and failures.

"Let our self-love be the power that changes the dream of our life...With this new power in our hearts, the power of self-love, let us transform every relationship we have, beginning with the relationship with ourselves. Help us to be free of conflict with others. Let us be happy to share our time with our loved ones and to forgive them for any injustice we feel in our mind. Help us to accept others just the way they are, without judgment."

Don Miguel Ruiz

Reflections
1. Is it difficult for us to admit when we're wrong or say we're sorry when we've made a mistake? Why or why not?
2. In one of our closest family of friendship relationships is one of us more likely to say that we're wrong than the other?
3. Think about one of our present or past supervisors who did take responsibility for their own actions, didn't have to always be right and could admit their mistakes. How did/

does their behavior make us feel?

4. Remember a time when we were on the wrong side of an argument and admitted it, how did it make us feel? What was the reaction of the other person?

Recommended Readings

1. Don Miguel Ruiz's book, <u>The Mastery of Love</u>, speaks to the need for us to love ourselves first.

2. Dr. Stephen Covey's book, <u>Principle-Centered Leadership</u>, writes that healthy people and organizations are those who are proactive. He includes Dr. Deming's fourteen points on quality in his foundation premise.

MAY YOU FEEL THE WARMTH OF MY HUG

CHAPTER 11

GUIDELINE 9
"BEING POSITIVE IS PERSONALLY POWERFUL"

"Reflect upon your present blessings, of which every man and woman has many; not on your past misfortunes of which all men [and women] have some."

Charles Dickens

<u>**Six Steps to Remaining Positive**</u>

Put a smile on our day and we feel good. Put a smile on someone else's day and we both feel great, then the two of us can make two others' lives shine a little brighter and we've begun to change the group, department, organization, family and so on—PERSON-SHINE at work.

Putting our "positive best" forward will give others support, help build morale and give us light to see the good in our work, our community and our home. Positive living and working means that we search for the bright side in all situations and provide the words and actions that will improve them. The following steps will help us remain positive each day:

1. Recognize and appreciate the blessings in our lives, our special talents and gifts and the goodness in those around us.
2. Think consciously about and admit to ourselves how we really feel each day.
3. Decide what "face" we want to show the world each day.
4. State, orally or in writing, how we want to behave that day.
5. Go into the world and do our best. Avoid self-judgment, self-abuse and regret.
6. Review the day and celebrate the positive successes we have experienced in implementing the behavior we decided on in the morning.

Positive Heroes

Michael J. Fox and Mattie J. Stephanek, both struck with life-taking diseases, understand the power of living positively. Michael J. Fox said that the last ten years of living with a serious illness have "been the best years of my life." It made him see clearly the good in his world. Mattie J. Stepanek had muscular dystrophy from an early age, but had special a gift of making others appreciate their blessings. Both remained positive while dealing with their serous situations. They proved to us that no matter how high the mountain or how rough the road, we can remain positive.

Victor Frankl, noted psychologist and proponent of positive living said about those living in a German Concentration camp, "They taught us that everything can be taken from a man, but one thing which is the last of human freedoms—to choose one's attitude in any given set of circumstances." These teachings can be applied to our everyday lives in several ways. Albert Einstein said, *"There are two ways to live our lives. One is as though nothing is a miracle. The other is as though everything is a miracle."*

Positive Living Questions/Decisions

How we view the world around us as well as our life experiences can give us greater power for living a rich joyful life rather than a depressing one. It is possible but not always easy to live this way. Perhaps we should look at the glass as being half full, rather than half-empty and then make a commitment to behave more positively each and every day. Even our heroes continuously seek improvement. They have difficult days in dealing with their challenges, but they are focused on and committed to living a positive life, because they know that it's a powerful way to live. Remember, positivism is energy producing and negativism is energy draining!

Each day we have a decision to make. It is our choice how we are going to live that day. How we are going to treat those we meet, live, and work with. It is a conscious decision that we must ask ourselves. Do we want to make the world smile? Do we want to bring sunshine into others' lives? We realize that we'll personally benefit greatly by how we behave towards others. Then we need to ask the next question, "how are we going to do this?" All of the Person-Shine guidelines, well practiced, will produce positive results. Use them wisely to focus your life on positive living and working.

The Silver Lining

Many people are faced with many tragedies. I call it the pioneering spirit. They were simply living their lives the best that they knew how and always looked for the sunshine. My mother, currently age ninety-five, and my father who died a few years ago, always said, "things could be worse." I often wondered if it came from a positive approach dealing with their childhood. My father suffered from an abusive father. His mother died when he was only four years old, so he grew up with much negativism around him. Likewise I had to deal with adversity during a four-year period when I was ages eleven to fifteen, a series of tragedies befell my family. First, my older brother was diagnosed with brittle-diabetes which meant, in his case a short lifespan, (dying when he was thirty-five) losing circulation throughout his body and other serious complications. Second, my mother was run over by a milk truck in front of our neighbors and disabled for life. The truck owner had little insurance for the medical bills. Third, our home burned down three days after my mother was injured. We had no insurance on the house. The livestock had to be sold and my family moved closer to town so mom could come home from the hospital from time to time. Fourth, we moved into a chicken coop while dad bought and moved a house onto the old foundation. Dad purchased a few head of cattle. It turned out one of the cows was diseased, which contaminated the entire herd, and they had to be destroyed. My parents never blamed anyone, including God, for their misfortunes.

Mom is still convinced that she is going to win the lottery, leave the nursing home and build a home in the woods. I believe that my mom and dad remained positive and strong because of their love for each other, their work ethic, their love for their friends and families, their faith in God and belief in the goodness of man! Remaining positive about life seemed to give them the strength to go on!

They always looked for the "silver lining" in everything. They found some sunshine in every day. They always counted their blessings and looked for the rainbow to appear!

Making a Positive Difference in Others' Lives

The people who make a difference in our lives are not necessarily the ones with the most credentials, the most money, or the most awards. They are the ones who care, the ones who most likely have made a positive difference in the lives of others.

A tenth grade teacher asked my class to write a poem. I created several verses about the flag and turned it in. A few weeks went by and the teacher returned the poem to me, with the following note on it. "Ken, this is good. May I include it in this year's all-school book of poems? You are good at expressing yourself and should consider doing more writing." This one teacher made me believe that I could write. It was a deciding moment in my life. I firmly believe that it was because of her that I had the courage to become an author, complete higher education and hold responsible leadership positions. She inspired me to believe that my innermost and strongest specialness is to openly and warmly, express myself. This one person made a difference in my life because she looked for the special strength in each student, much like my graduate school advisor, Dr. Richard Ashmun. That tenth grade teacher always put a smile on her day and a smile on my day – she exhibited strong positive living behaviors and made a positive difference in the life of others!

Joy-Stealers

To remain positive through life is to know joy, to feel joy! However it's not easy to remain joyful. To have joy—or be more joyful—we must understand better the forces that keep joy from us...the main *joy-stealers.*

They are:
1. *Circumstances*—illness, loss of loved ones, confinement, divorce, imprisonment and so on.
2. *People*—some people are just plain ornery, bad tempered and nasty. Put trust in them and they can let us down.
3. *Things*—sometimes things are a real burden just to have them around…breaking down, rot, rust, cost of maintaining or storing.
4. *Worry*—over what has happened or might happen drains energy and sabatoges hope.

Warren Wiersbe (from <u>Be Joyful</u>)

Being Forever Positive

Some say that it isn't possible always to be positive. Some say that sometimes, we have to do or say negative things. The research shows that in every situation it is possible to find a positive way to deal with it—even with all of the *joy-stealers* facing us. It doesn't mean that we can always be smiling and "gushy, gushy" happy. It doesn't mean that we have to be false about how we feel. It means that we can usually find a way to be positive, seeing positivism as a strength, rather than a weakness.

I truly believe that most people want to be positive, but life's experiences have been a burden making it difficult for them to be positive. However, there is great hope even for them to learn to lead a positive life. We all have our good days and our bad days, our good years and our bad years. We just need some help to find and use the "tools" that will help us be more positive every day–THE PERSON-SHINE GUIDELINES!

We need to remember that we are travelers on a journey of becoming and that we all need help on our journey. We each have the power to help others on their journey. We can help others' stars to shine. "*What lies behind us and what lies before us are tiny matters compared to what lies within us*"(Ralph Waldo Emerson).

"The richness of the human experience would lose something of rewarding joy if there were no limitations to overcome."

Helen Keller

Reflections
1. Can we think about and list what behaviors in ourselves or others, cause our hearts to smile.
2. Consider that what the caterpillar thinks is the end of the world, the butterfly knows is only the beginning. Do we

want to be a caterpillar or a butterfly? Why?

3. Why do so many people who have critical illnesses seem so at peace? Why do we feel better after spending time with them?

4. View a painting that we really love and reflecting on the artist's message. Can we write out the positive messages being conveyed?

5. Can we now apply the six steps for remaining positive for a week? Where should we place them to remind us daily of our intentions?

Recommended Readings

1. See Covey's <u>Principle-Centered Leadership</u> referenced in the last chapter. Read about his thirty methods of influence.

CHAPTER 12

GUIDELINE 10
"CARE ABOUT OTHERS' WHOLE LIVES"

"If I can stop one heart from breaking / I shall not live in vain."

Emily Dickinson

Caring About Others' Whole Lives

We need to get to know, really know, the people around us—our families, our neighbors, and our coworkers. This means knowing the whole lives of as many people as possible and keeping up to date on their lives by asking questions, keeping notes, seeking out our neighbors, contacting our colleagues and letting them know that we sincerely care about them. Things that we can do include remembering their birthdays and other happy occasions, supporting them when they are sick, celebrating personal accomplishments, and remembering other happy events that show caring for the whole life of the other person. We are busy, and yes it is a sacrifice, but it is needed. *We need to make the time!*

Caring about others' whole lives is so important. However, we need to acknowledge that it is often difficult. Our lives get busier and busier, and more complicated. It gets harder and harder to do. It does help us to remember that *sacrifice is good to the giver and to the recipient!* In Mitch Albom's book, <u>The Five People You Meet In Heaven</u>, the main character, Eddie, meets a soldier as one of his five people. The soldier was killed going back to save Eddie who had delayed his colleagues from leaving an area. The captain said, "Sacrifice is a part of life. It's supposed to be. It's not something to regret. It's something to aspire to. Little sacrifices. And big sacrifices. A mother works so her son can go to school. A daughter moves home to take care of her sick father." So we need to recognize that we are busy, it is difficult to sacrifice part or all of our schedule or activity to serve someone's need—to care about others' whole lives. But it is so very important to those helped, as well as the helper.

Caring is About Helping People Feel They Belong

We must tell and show people how we really feel about them. There is much evidence pointing to the need to communicate with one another. It's a skill or action which takes practice, based on building a trust relationship, and making a commitment to better express ourselves to others.

People want to belong. They want to be accepted. John O'Donohue, author of <u>Eternal Echoes – Exploring Our Yearning to Belong</u>, writes that we want to belong from the day that we're born until the day we die. This guideline is about belonging–we can help others feel, believe and know that they belong. In addition, it pertains to supporting someone who is seriously ill, celebrating others' accomplishments, special days and specialness. Its truly caring about the *whole person*!—their hurts, desires, needs, plans and so on.

Ray so Wanted his Friends to Talk to Him

Ray, a dear friend of mine passed away a year ago. Diagnosed with lung cancer when I asked him what bothered him the most since his diagnosis, he replied, "people, even some of my close friends don't call. Sometimes I feel they even try to avoid me by walking on the other side of the street. And when they do come into contact with me they seem so uncomfortable! Sometimes I want to scream at them that I am the same person I was before the diagnosis. I *do* want to talk about my disease–just ask me, really talk to me!" He obviously felt that he no longer belonged. This tells us that we need to take the time to care–to find out about our friends, families, and colleagues whole lives. In this reference and many others we should make the effort to ask the second question and let the other person make the decision as to how to respond...let the other person say, "No." No matter how impossible our question or request is, we should not assume that we know what their response will be. *Caring people have hearing hearts!*

Letting People Know that They are Important to us Brightens Their Worlds

Life's lessons are often behavior changing for us. During a very difficult three-year period in our lives, my wife and I were dramatically reminded of the importance of caring about the whole lives of others. So many people let us know that they supported us, still cared about us, and were still our friends. They did this by calling, stopping in, praying for us, sending notes and directly asking us to talk about how we were doing. This continued throughout the three years and made an impact on us that changed us forever. These people never let us feel alone–that we didn't belong.

Shortly thereafter, we moved to another town and to a new job. During my first week at work, at an all company meeting, the president of the institution handed out years of service certificates. The next day I dictated memos to all those people telling them how good they must feel about having touched others lives for those years. I received a positive note back from one person who was honored: "Ken Mills, I don't know you and don't know why you sent me this celebration note, but it is the first time in my twenty plus years with this organization that anyone has even used my name, let alone sent me such a note. Your note reached me on an ordinary day and made it very extraordinary. Thank you!" Since then, I have sent over 2000 cards, notes and letters a year! My wife and I continue to let people know we care about them, their "whole lives," which means that they know they are forever in our thoughts and prayers. It is such a powerful way of letting others know how much we care and that they "belong" in our world.

Some Days it's Hard to See the Sunshine

Sometimes in our lives, life just seems so hard, so difficult! About ten years ago, I remember my dad asking me. "Why is life always so hard for us?" He and mom were about eighty-three years old at the time and mom had just had another setback. She was in the hospital waiting for surgery. They had suffered many tragedies in their lifetime. This question came from a man who had lived through so much tragedy and yet never let the negative get him down. He had lost a son, his house burned down, his wife had been run over by a truck, and he lost herds of animals to diseases. I remember him being only positive, always finding the rainbow. I was thankful that I could be there for him, at that moment, as tears welled up in his eyes. He had always been there for me. When we got to the floor my mom was on, his smile came back and he said, "things will get better. Amelia will come back from surgery just as she has all the rest of the times," and she did. *There are times when life is just so very hard to deal with. That is why we need each other, why we need to have someone to lean on and why it's so important for us all to work on caring about others' whole lives.* I was thankful that I was there for dad at that moment. But if I hadn't been, how wonderful it would have been if someone near had seen a tear in his eye and said, "Harlem, what's wrong? I care! Lean on me a bit!"

Letting People Know We Care

Over the years, I have collected material from interviews, media reports, seminars, and other research sources dealing with how we can let people know that we care about them. I have shared this list with others and been told that they used it to set personal/professional goals to improve their support of families, friends and coworkers.

- Take time to develop personal relationships with coworkers.

- Learn ways to create meaningful connections.

- Find common interests in and with others.

- Find out what excites/motivates those around you.

- Recognize the balance of family life, work life, leisure life and spiritual life.

- Include staff's families in company events.

- Find out about family–children, spouses, relatives.

- Publish Bios with photos of new employees.

- Ask people the second question after, "How are you?" and getting the typical "I'm Fine," ask, "No, I really want to know...How are you?"

- Visit those who are sick and find out how they are really feeling, thinking and coping with their condition–call, send cards and notes of support or celebration whenever we think they are needed–we'll never do it too much.

Everyone Can do Something
No gesture, when given with the pure intention of caring about someone's whole life, is too small. William Wordsworth said, "*Small service is true service while it lasts: / of humblest friends, bright creature, scorn not one....*"

Remember we can bring sunshine to someone's life, give them a rainbow of hope and let them know that they are not alone, that they belong and are important to others. We all have the power to do wonderful things that may not cost much money nor take much time. *It is our choice!* If we are present to others, our presence becomes a *gift* and our moments of affirmation will help build esteem.

> *"Do what you can to show you care about other people and you will make our world a better place."*
>
> **Rosalyn Carter**

Reflections

1. How did we feel at a time when we were low from life's challenges, perhaps wondering if anyone cared, and then received a much appreciated call inviting us out to coffee or dinner?

2. What is the best place for open sharing with family or friends? For example in crisis, restaurants, home, cars, walks in the woods or strolls by a lake.

3. Can we remember a time when we made a rainbow visit to a friend who was in crisis? Maybe we even saw the rainbow in their eyes as we entered the room, or gave them a hug—held it for awhile—and said, "I care. I want to help."

4. How can we show our coworkers that we really care about their whole lives?

MAY THIS HUG SPRINKLE STARDUST ON YOUR DAY

CHAPTER 13

GUIDELINE 11
"VERBALIZE YOUR FEELINGS, VISUALIZE YOUR THOUGHTS"

"Be impeccable with your words. Speak with integrity. Say only what you mean."

Don Miguel Ruiz

The Guideline

This guideline is about the matter of expressing ourselves. We hear people say that person "X" knows how I feel about them, I don't need to tell them; or I have this special relationship with person "Y" and I don't have to tell them how I feel. Rather, we should tell and show people how we feel about them in positive ways. There is much evidence to support the need to improve communication with one another. It is a skill that can be learned and practiced. If we truly value the people in our lives then we should make a commitment to express ourselves more and more often to others—in positive ways. We strive to build a trust relationship based on a mutual need for understanding one another—where they are?

Gifts from Others' Tragedies

Consider the Shuttle Columbia tragedy on Saturday February 1, 2003, the doomed flights of 9-11, the Challenger in 1996 and the miners in 2003, who had all but given up and were miraculously rescued. Common powerful, personal messages came from the survivors and loved ones—survivors of these and other tragedies:

- Never let a day pass without telling your loved ones that you love them.
- Never let the sun go down without settling a quarrel.
- Never put aside the urge, no matter how busy the day, to find a way to help someone in need—family, friend, neighbor or stranger.
- Never allow hate to make a permanent home in your heart. Find a way to get rid of it, usually by putting ego aside and placing others first.

Why do we allow ourselves to forget these powerful important messages in our day to day lives? Because we are human! Those who have died or otherwise directly suffered from these and other tragedies have given us immense gifts, dramatically reminding us how fragile life is. We need to appreciate life, to be thankful for our blessings, have a renewed commitment to reach out to others and to never forget those who have positively touched our lives.

In newspapers, magazines, radio and television interviews we have read and heard people from all walks of life talk about how they reacted after hearing about these tragedies. They said that in so doing they felt that they were closer to the victims and that they were helping them in some way by doing something for someone else. They also said that it helped the hurt they felt for the victims, i.e. it helped them grieve.

We can learn so much, be reminded of so many things, by listening to and watching others go through some kind of serious life challenge. We may offer our prayers and thoughts on their behalf, and want them to know that we care and their losses are not in vain. Their coping experiences have enriched the lives of many people, reminding them of their blessings, the goodness of God and the value of life.

May we see the miracles around us, life's abounding treasures, and find mental sunshine in our lives each day. May we give thanks to those who, in their suffering, have opened their hearts and minds, giving sunshine to others.

Life's Tragedies can be Barriers to Expressing our Feelings

My hero and my only brother died at the age of thirty-five. He had been a brittle-diabetic since childhood. When he was thirty-five his health complications forced him to go on dialysis. He had little income and no insurance. In order to begin the dialysis, he had to agree to be in an experimental research program at the University of Minnesota. At 3 a.m. one cold winter night he received a call to go to the University. They had a donor for him.

That very night he and his wife traveled three hours from northern Minnesota to Minneapolis. He was the seventh pancreas/kidney transplant patient in Minnesota but it wasn't successful and on Christmas day, after his little girls of five and seven kissed their daddy goodbye, he died. After a time they moved to southern Minnesota where their mother went to college and became an RN. Later on their mother became chemically dependent. The girls were not able to grieve the loss of their dad.

Ten years later my wife and I received a letter from her telling us about her chemical dependency. By now she was in a "tough love" chemical dependent unit in Grand Forks. We called her and she said that we could visit her the next weekend on family day. Shortly after I arrived she told me that she had just received a call from her oldest daughter's high school counselor stating that he believed that she was also chemically dependent. To my surprise I was invited to sit in "group session" where the daughter was going to be the target of the group intervention. After trying to get her to respond to the group's deep probing for an hour, her only response was tears rolling down her cheeks. No words!

Over the next few years she went through two "tough love" units, had a baby and began to heal. One time during those years she wrote me a letter saying, "I know that the family is probably wondering why I don't share my feelings at family gatherings when everyone is asked to share what they are most thankful for or appreciate. The reason is that I can't talk without crying, because whenever I try I think of my dad and I can't stop crying. I'll get better. But for now, please tell the family." She did become healed, graduated from college with honors and is a wonderful mom and a very successful business woman. Today she can stand in front of family and others to share her feelings and emotions. She learned it is all right, more healthy, to express feelings. She had not been able to grieve her dad's death. She had been put in an emotional prison. But now she is a new person! She has grown and matured, freed up from the bonds of those early deep hurts and pains.

Our experiences may hamper our ability to freely express feelings. HOWEVER, THAT DOES NOT MEAN THAT WE CANNOT FIND WAYS TO LEARN HOW TO OVERCOME THOSE BARRIERS AND SHARE OUR EMOTIONS, ESPECIALLY TOWARD THOSE WE CARE ABOUT AND LOVE THE MOST.

Ah, to have a feeling, to think a thought, to dream a dream are powers of the mind, but if we can't express those to others...Or they theirs to us, then what's the good for it's mankind that's on this earth...And so we must be able to communicate those feelings, thoughts and dreams if we are to have true peace and real joy...And love...And the same to others...To not be able to do so would be like the artist having no canvas, nor palette, so his creation would be imprisoned in his mind and heart forever.

Kenneth H. Mills

Reflections

1. How did we feel if we've ever tried to sit in a room with others and remain silent for a stated period of time?

2. Do we daily try to tell our loved ones how much they mean to us in some way?

3. Have we ever lost a friend due to an accident or disease and not been able to say goodbye? Why?

4. Consider being told that we have a very little time to live, who would we want to spend time with, who would we need to tell that we love them, who would we need to hold and who would we need to say goodbye to? If we have time to write one brief message about our life, what would we want to say?

CHAPTER 14

GUIDELINE 12
"CELEBRATE, APPLAUD AND REMEMBER"

"The most exquisite pleasure is giving pleasure to others."

Jean De La Bruyere

The Meaning of Celebration

What is a celebration? It can be as simple as mentioning someone's name as part of a greeting. It may be something we do at birthdays, other special days, like a family reunion that takes much planning. Webster says that it means "to observe, as a festival or an occasion to make known or famous...have a lively or happy time, rejoice, make merry...." Dr. John O'Donohue shares that,

> Celebration is one of the most intense and delightful forms of presence. Even a small event can be an excuse for a celebration...There is a sense of joy and happiness in celebration. When we celebrate, we joyfully acknowledge and recognize the presence of some person, thing or achievement that delights us...When we

celebrate we are taking the time to recognize, to open our eyes and behold in our life the quiet miracles and gifts that seek no attention; yet each day they nourish, shelter and animate our life.

Celebrating Our Day!

A note on our pillow, breakfast in bed, no chores for one day, surprises, balloons/decorations, a special coffee at work, a certain plate or cup by our place, cards, letters, calls and e-mails, and maybe sitting at the dinner table surrounded by family and friends! Perhaps we share a favorite dinner, a meal of our choice! Maybe someone even tells us why we are special, or recounts special memories about us. Then the cake arrives, candles flickering, as a loved one carries it in and places it before us. We hear "Happy Birthday" in many tones and are asked to make a wish and blow out the candles in one breath. We are given the first piece of cake, one of our choosing, and of course, it's the flavor that we requested. Life just doesn't get any better! All of this stops the world, our world, as we are told and shown that we are special, cared about and loved. It is our day. Some actually turn it into their week or month. Yes, others may have been born on our day, but to each person who is, it's also their day.

President Mark, of Progressive Communications (one of the Taylor Corporation Companies), tells us of a celebration practice at his company. "At our company we gather around the lunch table in the cafeteria and share what is special about the birthday person. This has proved to be more powerful than I ever expected."

What a gift it is to be reminded by others that they are pleased and thankful that we were born, and belong in their worlds. Brightening other worlds? Yes! People who do this for us influence our self-esteem, reinforce our self worth and strengthen our identity.

The Circle Of Life

We are born! We grow up learning, maturing, developing through life stages—kids, children, teenagers, young adults, maybe married adults and perhaps parents. And then, if we are really blessed, grandparents. *The circle of life!* Let's focus for a bit on grandparenting. People talk about and try to define grandparenting, but its impossible to capture the golden richness of new life until we live it and become grandparents. To describe the world of grandchildren and grandparents is like trying to describe a summer sunset, fall colors or rain drops on rose petals to someone who has never seen them. Grandparenting is a place where only gods, angels, kings and queens dwell, as those are what grandchildren crown them to be. They run to the royalty with open arms anxious to be swooped up and gently hugged. And when they speak, we remember the same words spoken by their moms and dads at an earlier time. Our hearts fill with joy as we share this love of being grandparents...I love you most of all daddy, I love you most of all mom, I love you most of all nana, I love you most of all poppa! The circle of life!

We take this moment to honor, celebrate and give thanks for these angels, these miracles of life that crown us with rays of perpetual sunshine, by their presence and their unconditional everlasting love, every moment of every day!...Our Grandchildren

Alex Theordoroff	*Hannah Mills*	*Madeline Mills*
Christina Theordoroff	*Sarah Mills*	*Tyler Mills*
Paul Theodoroff	*Emily Mills*	

Being Sensitive To The Celebrant

We need to be sensitive to situations and opportunities to celebrate. Sometimes it is difficult to celebrate someone, but we can find a way if we really try.

Frank lived in his hometown for over seventy-five years. He was the town leader, the real power broker. He did not want to be recognized for his many years of service as a community leader. He was a very humble person who never flaunted his power. It just came to him over the years. Now enter the CEO of a new organization. We'll call him Jack. He had been in town for about four years. Jack, through his organization's foundation, had mounted a successful fundraising campaign. In the process he had received Frank's blessings and considerable good counsel and Jack wanted to give back to Frank in some significant way. Person after person told him that Frank wouldn't hear of such a thing. It so happened that about this time the word got around that Frank was going to retire or at least withdraw from some of his major activities.

Jack met with Denny, a leading company and community leader, and Frank's good friend. In their discussion Jack said to Denny, "You and your fellow corporate presidents are great leaders and know that Frank is so deserving of honors, recognition and celebration. Yet, you're telling me that your great minds can't find a way to honor him that would be acceptable to him." Denny said, "Jack, people have tried and Frank's actually walked out of a surprise event, returned gifts and otherwise shown his anger." Jack replied, "All that tells me is that you haven't found the right way to do it!" A few weeks passed and one day Jack's phone rang. The voice on the other end said, "Jack, this is Denny. I left you that day and thought and thought about our discussion. The other night I got together with Fred and Frank's other closest friends and told them about our conversation. We finally agreed on one way to honor Frank that seemed to be a winner. We could honor Frank by each year honoring a student with a scholarship, given in Frank's name." He accepted the idea! And so annually a scholarship award is given out to that student who demonstrates the most potential for community leadership. And each commencement booklet carries a story about Frank's contributions to and leadership in the community. His name and life will be celebrated forever!

<u>Several Ways To Celebrate</u>

Celebrating others frequently, sincerely and respectfully in a variety of ways can raise their self-esteem. It makes them feel that they belong in a relationship, a group of some kind, a family, a department or a neighborhood. We can stop or enhance others' worlds by recognizing them. The following are some of the ways people have said that they celebrated others:

- **Remembering and using their names.**
- **Closing the space between others and us with handshakes, hugs or other positive body language.**
- **Recognizing events and accomplishments of others by sending news clippings announcing their events, calling them or sending them notes.**
- **Randomly inviting people for dinner, lunch or just coffee, saying, "I just want to hear about what's going on in your life."**
- **Sending cards at holidays, birthdays, anniversaries, years of service and so on.**
- **Picking someone you know and calling five people asking them to send this person a card wishing them a sunshine day in some way.**
- **Recognizing children's school performance, not only when they have A's and B's, but also when they've tried very hard, put in much effort and only got C's or D's.**

Celebration is one way to brighten others' worlds. It is very powerful to honor others, celebrate their specialness, recognize their contributions or even just mention their name.

Who should we celebrate today, tonight or tomorrow? *May we feel the power and joy of celebration in our life…by receiving it and giving it!*

One way to uplift the spirit is to celebrate any and all the good there is for it delights the soul!

Kenneth H. Mills

Reflections

1. What is the best way to celebrate our love partners? Do we so honor them?
2. Are there co-workers who deserve to be, but haven't been honored? What should we do about it?
3. How do we respond when people respectfully use our names...be they friends, family or strangers? Do we use others' names, rather then merely saying hello, goodbye, how are you and so on?
4. Do we believe in the power of celebration? If so, do we celebrate, stop/enhance people's worlds, enough?

CHAPTER 15

PERSON-SHINE JOURNEY...IT'S OUR CHOICE

"You give but little when you give of possessions. It is when you give of yourself that you truly give."
Kahlil Gibran

<u>**Person-Shine Summary**</u>

This book was written first to remind us of the power we have within us to make the world a better place in which to live. Second, it is intended to provide a pathway to show us how to use that power and brighten others' worlds. To set the stage for that pathway we must be aware of negative and positive forces in our lives, their impact on our lives and the commitment we need to make to using our inner sunshine power to brighten others' worlds. We introduced and defined a pathway called PERSON-SHINE, "THE POWER OF BRIGHTENING OUR LIVES". We read about its five characteristics: *caring, love, respect, dignity and sensitivity*—and the twelve Person-Shine Guidelines and accompanying stories and reflections.

We studied how to brighten the worlds of our love partners, our children, our coworkers, our neighbors, our friends and even strangers. Research and stories in several settings were shared that dealt with self-power topics such as celebration, choices, asking the second question, letting the other person say no, knowing our own specialness, managing our weaknesses, enhancing our strengths, and the power of one. A strong case was made for living a positive life and brightening others' worlds. However, it's up to each one of us. It's always our choice, whether or not we want to choose *this* journey.

The following stories are about individuals who chose the positive pathway.

The Waving Lady

The May 10, 2003, issue of <u>The Orlando Sentinel</u>, reported on a very special person named Jennie Blair. However, until this article was published hundreds, perhaps thousands, of people in the Orlando area knew her as the "waving lady." This forty-nine-year-old woman was paid $8.55 an hour to help children safely across the road. She had done this very well for over eleven years. However, she sees her world as much larger. She is a bringer of joy, a solver of problems, and a purveyor of good advice. The gloomy, the sleepy, the sad, all get words and actions of encouragement from the waving lady as they pass by. "Come on girlfriend, don't be sad." She makes a mock-sad face and does a little dance until the driver perks up. Sometimes, there are no words exchanged. Blair just blows kisses, or dances a little jig, or points her finger like a game-show host. She has a husband, four grown children and twelve grandchildren. She lives in a little place with a pink rose bush and a magnolia tree, and basketballs and tricycles in her yard. She had dreams of becoming a psychiatrist, which wasn't meant to be. However, she never gave up her dream, she just became the "counselor of the crosswalk." "Some kinda way, the Lord gave me a blessing to love other kids the way my parents loved me. I think the kids need me!" The kids say that it really helps them when she talks to them. Only one person has complained about her in all these years. A male driver called her supervisor and complained. The waving lady said, "If he wants me to stop waving at him, he'll need to drive another road. I know that I can't work out there forever, I'll give'm twenty-seven years, and then I'm going to quit. Then I'm going to be my own boss and come out here and work for free."

Susan Vreeland, Learning How to Help Others in Need

Susan Vreeland wrote the best seller, <u>The Girl in Hyacinth Blue</u>, while fighting cancer. When people learn of others' misfortunes or illnesses they toss out the common phrase, "If you need anything, just let me know." They want to do something, but don't know what to do or how to do it. Susan believes that we should not ask, as the person needing help may not know how to tell us, but instead we should plunge ahead and do something. "When I was diagnosed with cancer many people, some that I barely knew or didn't know at all, sent me books and articles and did many things for me. Each act lifted me." Each act let her know that she was not alone. She came to realize that she was humbled by all of the acts and gifts. The giver's actions were transforming them to high positive emotional places! The giving continues and she says, "I'm thankful that now I can be the one giving. My oncologist puts me in contact with his patients to help quell their fears, give practical advice and offer hope by example." Susan is practicing what we call "Paying it forward" in earlier chapters. We don't have to do the grand gestures to heal the world. It can happen one person at a time. Mother Teresa says, "We can do no great things—only small things with great love."

Make a Difference Day

Many examples like this are highlighted each year during the annual "Make a Difference Day" in the fall. It is cosponsored by USA Weekend Magazine and the Points of Light Foundation. There are also examples of people helping people such as the kindness movement where students and people across the community learn about and are encouraged to do and talk about random acts of kindness. The reason for

112

doing this, of course, is not to leave to chance that people will take the time and make the effort to help others. These community wide efforts remind us what we already know and should do, but perhaps don't do as much as we should.

Operation Pocket Change

John T. McCann, a teacher's aide at Howard Middle School in Orlando, Florida, shared this story about a teacher who is powerfully patriotic and always believes that she can make a positive difference. After the war on Iraq broke out, she was heard on the schools public address system talking about operation pocket change, a drive to collect and send goodies to the troops. She had students from classroom to classroom gathering such items as spare change, toothpaste, sunflower seeds, anything that could withstand a voyage to our soldiers in the Middle East. When Mrs. C, as John calls her, showed up at the post office with enough money to send only forty-six of the fifty care packages, one of the postal workers offered to help pay for the other four. Another worker chipped in, then another, plus two customers. Mrs. C said, "It just makes you feel good about people." So here's to small seeds sown that yield bountiful harvests.

Truly Giving a Part of Herself

The last story gives us one of the easiest—but perhaps most difficult—ways to practice our person-shine behaviors. Jennifer's story was reported in the June 3, 2003, issue of The Milwaukee Journal. Jennifer is a thirty-three-year-old lawyer who gave a portion of her liver so that her uncle could live. He was running out of time and apparently low on the donor needed list. She suffered much during the transplant operation, but she survived. The reporter commented that "Jennifer has every quality of heart, spirit, mind and body that a woman could want. She wanted this article written, not to talk about her courage, but to encourage others to have the 'guts' to donate their organs. More then 80,000 Americans are on waiting lists for organ donations and most will never get them." Maybe this article will help save one or more lives because it gave someone the awareness or courage to be a donor. One donor can save up to eight lives! The reporter said that she had never even signed a donor card before, but since her niece's actions, last Friday, on her brother's (the one who received Jennifer's donation) birthday, "I got the card, filled it out, signed it and now carry it in my purse."

There are a million such stories. We all have at least one. The beautiful part of brightening others' worlds is that the act or acts may be as simple as the waving lady's mission or as difficult and complex as donating one's organs. But both actions are equally and immensely important to the recipients, as well as to those who hear about them.

May we be committed to know our specialness, celebrate it and use it to make a positive difference in someone else's world each day. The gift may be a smile, a word, a gesture or some unselfish act of kindness. Regardless of the behavior, we can be certain that it will make other, and our, heartlights to shine!

...And make the world a better place. Each act that we experience on our life journey, will help us compose our heartsong and make it a symphony of joy and love.

May we feel the sunshine support of others when we are in difficult times. May we choose to use the power within us to "brighten others' worlds" every day of our life!

You are invited to join us on our person-shine journey!

I leave you, the reader, with the following words of hope and challenge. If we can each try to bring more sunshine to our brothers and sisters of this earth, then we can brighten the entire world!

Brotherhood of Heroes

A candle burns brightly
It's glow radiates throughout the world
...And some can see.
For heartsight is only hampered by human barriers
But enhanced by God's Blessings...
Fueled by belief and good works.

Open our eyes, if we care,
And the brotherhood of heroes
Will see the candle burning.
As it's flame grows brighter, it will penetrate
The closets of our minds, allowing in sunshine
That will heal hearts and brighten worlds.

Kenneth H. Mills

Reflections

1. In developing a set of goals/activities for our Person-Shine Journey, what might we want to focus on? What guidelines touched us the most?
2. In celebrating our strengths, which of the guidelines would match our strengths the best?
3. How might we use the Person-Shine Guidelines and Characteristics in our workplace?
4. Could we name five people that we would want to share and discuss the Person-Shine Guidelines with?

APPENDICES

Appendix A: Panel of Experts

Karla Flak, Publisher
Carol Freed, President's Assistant
Mary Herzog, Administrative Assistant
Lori B. Knitt RN, BSN
Dr. Patrick Lacey, Vice President, Learning
Darlene Ann (Hanson) Mills, RN, Design
    Consultant
James Pierce, Dean Business and Marketing
    (ret.)
Kristine Pierce, Executive Trainer
Susan Pierce, Business Development Manager
Dr. Mary Kay Rudolph
Ann Splinter, Marketing and Public Relations
    Director
Pamela K. Taylor, MS Ed. Counseling
Kim Theodoroff, BA Business Management
Mary Theodoroff. RN, BSN

Appendix B:
Reviewers

Dr. Richard Ashmun, Professor Emeritus,
Marketing Education, University of
Minnesota

Dr. John Bailey, Professor Emeritus, Carthage
College

Glenn Gabriel, Director of Operations

Tom Hanson, DDS

Don Kastello, Business Developer

Jennifer Mills

Kenneth J. Mills, Educator, BA Psychology,
MA Psychology, Economics & English.

Mark Mills, President, Progressive
Communications

Dr Judith E. Paul, Professor Emeritus,
Business and Accounting, University of
Wisconsin—Platteville

Appendix C:

Person-Shine Story Submission Procedures.

Anyone wishing to submit true stories representing one or more of the Person-Shine Guidelines may send them to: Person-Shine Guideline Stories, P.O Box 421, Sheboygan, WI 53082.

The stories should be no more then one page, single spaced, typed (maximum font size 12) and should be stories that the author has experienced or observed first-hand so they can attest to their accuracy and truthfulness.

The one page story should be sent with this signed page: To the best of my knowledge this is a true story. I understand that it may appear in part or in whole in future editions of Person-Shine. I give my permission to have it included as is or edited to fit the format and content of the book. I understand that I will not receive any compensation for its appearance in any future editions.

Name (signature)_____

Name (typed or printed) _____

Address_____

City, State & zip_____

Tel. # (H)_____   (C)_____

E-mail: _____

Appendix D:
Illustration
and Design Team

Troy & Lisa Anderson, White Ivy Design
Lori B. Knitt
Darlene Ann (Hanson) Mills
Kristine Pierce
Mary Theodoroff

Appendix E: Hugs Logo Order Blank

Mail to : Person-Shine
P.O. Bx 421
Sheboygan, Wi 53082

Please Send _____ Bags (two sets per bag of the hugs logo sticker pages which appear at the end of this book at a cost of $5.00 per bag.) Please add $1.50 for postage and handling.

I have enclosed a check or money order for $_____ to cover the cost of the bags and postage and handling.

TO: _____

_____

_____

_____

E-mail_____

Phone_____

Appendix F.
Reference List

Rafael Aguayo, <u>Dr. Deming</u>, Fireside (New York:Simon & Schuster, 1990).

Mitch Albom, <u>The Five People You Meet In Heaven</u>, (New York:Hyperion, 2003).

Mitch Albom, <u>Tuesdays With Morrie</u>, (New York:Hyperion, 2001).

Marcus Buckingham & Donald Clifton, Ph.D., <u>Now, Discover Your Strengths</u>, (New York:The Free Press, 2001).

William C. Byham, Ph.D., <u>Zapp—The Lightning of Empowerment</u>, (United States:DDI Press, 1988).

Jack Canfield, Mark Victor Hansen, & Heather McNamara, <u>Chicken Soup for the Unsinkable Soul</u>, (Florida:Health Communications, Inc., 1999).

Jack Canfield, Mark Victor Hansen & Bud Gardner, <u>Chicken Soup for the Writer's Soul</u>, (Florida:Health Communications, Inc., 2000).

Gary Chapman, <u>The Five Love Languages—How to Express Heartfelt Commitment to Your Mate</u>, (Chicago:Northfield Publishing, 1995).

John Cook, <u>The Book of Positive Quotations</u>, (Minneapolis:Fairview Press, 1997).

Stephen R. Covey, <u>Principle-Centered Leadership</u>, (New York:Fireside—Simon & Schuster, 1992).

Stephen R. Covey, <u>The 7 Habits of Highly Effective Families</u>, (New York:Franklin Covey Company—Golden Books, 1997).

Emily Dickinson, <u>Collected Poems</u>, (New York:Barnes & Noble Books, 1993).

Marc Gafni, <u>Soul Prints—Your Path to Fulfillment</u>, (New York:Pocket Books, 2001).

Shakti Gawain, <u>Creative Visualization</u>, (California:Nataraj Publishing—New World Library, 2002).

Rudolph W. Giuliani, <u>Leadership</u>, (New York:Miramax Books, 2002).

Rudolph W. Giuliani, <u>Leadership Through the Ages</u>, (New York: Miramax, 2002).

Spencer Johnson, M.D., <u>Who Moved My Cheese</u>, (New York:G. P. Putnam's Sons, 1998).

Steven Dale Jones, Bobby Tomberlin & Diamond Rio, <u>One More Day—Making Every Day Count</u>, (Nashville:Rutledge Hill Press, 2002).

Jeffrey A. Krames, <u>What the Best CEOS Know—7 Exceptional leaders & Their Lessons for Transforming any Business</u>, (New York:McGraw-Hill Companies, Inc., 2003).

Stephen C. Lundin, Ph.D., Harry Paul and John Christensen, <u>Fish—A Remarkable</u>

<u>Way to Boost Morale and Improve Results</u>, (New York:Hyperion, 2000).

John O'Donohue, <u>Eternal Echoes—Exploring Our Yearning To Belong</u>, (New York:HarperCollins Publishers, Inc., 1999).

Don Miguel Ruiz, <u>The Four Agreements</u>, (California:Amber-Allen Publishing, 1997).

Don Miguel Ruiz, <u>The Mastery of Love</u>, (California:Amber-Allen Publishing, 1999).

Ronald Steel, <u>In Love with Night </u>(New York: Simon & Schuster, 2000).

Rick Warren, <u>The Purpose Driven Life</u>, (Zondervan:Grand Rapids, Michigan, 2002).

The "hugs logos" on the following six pages are samples of messages that we can attach to memos, letters, other correspondence and gifts. Additional hugs logos may be ordered using the order form in Appendix E.

Notes

Notes

Notes

A HUG HEALS A BROKEN HEART

A HUG SAYS I'M SORRY

THANKS FOR BEING THERE FOR ME

YOU ARE SPECIAL

A HUG HELPS YOU THRU THE DAY

THANKS FOR BEING A PART OF MY LIFE

I'M HERE FOR YOU

A HUG MEANS THAT YOU BELONG

I CARE ABOUT YOU

YOU ARE VERY IMPORTANT

MAY YOU FEEL MY SUPPORT

FEEL THE WARMTH & STRENGTH

THANKS FOR BEING A PART OF MY LIFE

A HUG HEALS

I LOVE YOU JUST THE WAY YOU ARE

FASSON®

FasTrack® BRAND

PRESSURE SENSITIVE PAPER

AnswerLine
1-800-443-9380

PERMANENT

FASSON®

FasTrack® BRAND

PRESSURE SENSITIVE PAPER

AnswerLine
1-800-443-9380

PERMANENT

FASSON®

FasTrack® BRAND

PRESSURE SENSITIVE PAPER

AnswerLine
1-800-443-9380

PERMANENT

FASSON®

FasTrack® BRAND

PRESSURE SENSITIVE PAPER

AnswerLine
1-800-443-9380

PERMANENT

FASSON®

FasTrack® BRAND

PRESSURE SENSITIVE PAPER

AnswerLine
1-800-443-9380

PERMANENT

FASSON®

FasTrack® BRAND

THE POWER OF HUGS IS MIGHTY

A HUG IS SUNSHINE TO THE HEART

MAY YOU FEEL THE WARMTH OF MY HUG

A HUG SAYS "I CARE"

MAY YOU FEEL MY HEARTSENT HUG

THANK YOU FOR BEING MY FRIEND

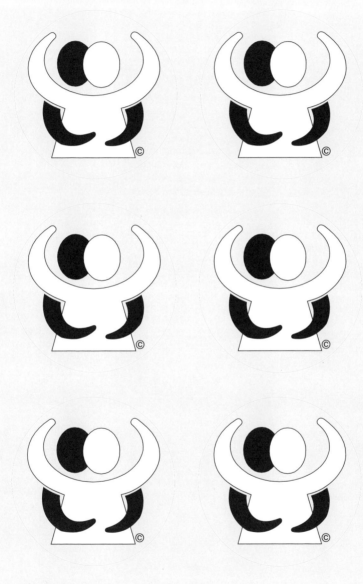